Al-'Ubudiyyah
Being a True Slave of Allah

Shaykh al-Islam Ibn Taymiyah

Translated by: Nasiruddin al-Khattab

Ta-Ha Publishers Ltd.

Published by:
Ta-Ha Publishers Ltd.
Unit 4, The Windsor Centre
Windsor Grove, West Norwood
London, SE27 9NT, UK
Website: www.tahapublishers.com
Email: support@tahapublishers.com

By: Shaykh al-Islam Ibn Taymiyah
Translated by: Nasiruddin al-Khattab
General Editor: Afsar Siddiqui

A catalogue record of this book is available from the British Library.

ISBN-13: 978 1897940 88 4

Printed and bound by: Mega Basim, Turkey

Cover/Book design and typeset by Shakir Abdulcadir.
www.OpenSquares.co.uk

Cover Photo by Shakir Abdulcadir

Contents

Translator's Foreword

There are major questions that human beings always ask and wonder about. Where did we come from? Where are we going? What are we doing here?

Philosophers and men of religion have tried to answer these questions. Some have suggested that there is no purpose to creation, or that the Creator created the universe and then forgot about it. Some others think that there is just one purpose in life: to pursue full enjoyment by indulging in sensual pleasures. Others believe that it is best to ignore these basic questions, and simply live day to day, taking life as it comes. Another idea is that there is a purpose to life, which is to attain perfection.

However, regardless of the answers people come up with to these basic questions, there is one goal that they all have in common: everyone is seeking happiness and fulfilment. The modern world we live in was, until recently, dominated by two major ideologies, capitalism and socialism/communism. Although their means were diametrically opposed, both shared the goal of achieving happiness and fulfilment. The socialist/communist systems collapsed, thus proving their failure to achieve materialistic fulfilment or even to meet the basic needs of individuals and societies. Their collapse also demonstrated how millions of people can be deceived by the ideology of a leadership that wants to assume the position of a "god", controlling people's lives and destiny. This collapse also exposed the immense misery of the masses who were subjected, willingly or otherwise, to these kinds of systems.

Another result of the collapse of these systems was that people saw this as vindication for the capitalist system. Capitalism does indeed fulfil the materialistic needs and wants of some, but only for the 15% or so who control some 85% of the world's resources and wealth. Capitalism may "work" for them, but it is at the expense of the third world countries, whose people are pushed ever deeper into poverty, misery, crisis, debt and hunger. The luxuries enjoyed by the few also come at the expense of nature and the environment, which surely cannot for much longer sustain the assaults of pollution, negligence and human greed.

In spite of this capitalist "success" and the relative material comfort available to people in the West, happiness and fulfilment still elude the people who live there – including the Muslims among them. Psychological problems abound, taking many forms, such as depression, anxiety, panic attacks, phobias, obsessive-compulsive behaviour, addictions, bipolar disorder ("manic depression"), paranoia, schizophrenia..., the list is seemingly endless. It is said that the cases of mental illness outnumber all other types of illness combined. Moreover, there are increasing signs that the capitalist system itself is also vulnerable to collapse.

Islam is not silent on these issues. It offers answers to those basic questions and addresses the issues of humanity's health, happiness and fulfilment. Once we know why we were created and what we are here for, we can focus on our life's purpose. This will bring us into harmony with ourselves and our existence, and the other pieces of life will fall into place, thus resolving many of the conflicts from which our malaise and "dis-ease" stem.

In this book, al-'Ubudiyyah, one of Islam's greatest scholars, Ibn Taymiyah, discusses the Islamic answers to the basic human questions in depth. He explains in detail the purpose of our existence, which is to be true slaves of Allah, making Him the focus of our love and attaining happiness and fulfilment by making Him our goal, Ibn Taymiyah tells us:

"The heart is inherently dependent on Allah in two ways: from the point of view of worship, which is the ultimate goal, and from the point of view of seeking His help and relying upon Him, which are the means to that end. The heart cannot be sound, or succeed, or find joy, or be happy, or feel pleasure, or be good, or be at peace, or find tranquillity, except by worshipping its Lord, loving Him and returning to Him. Even if it attains all that it can enjoy of created things, it will not feel at peace or find tranquillity, because it has an inherent need for its Lord, for He is the focus of its worship, love and seeking, and this is the only way to attain joy, happiness, pleasure, peace and tranquillity.

"...For if a person is helped to attain what he loves, seeks, desires and wants, but he does not worship Allah, he will never achieve anything but sorrow, regret and suffering. He can never be free of the pain and hardship of this life except through loving Allah sincerely, so that Allah becomes his ultimate desire and he loves Him for what He is, and he loves anyone or anything else only for His sake, and he does not love anything for its own sake except Allah. If he does not achieve this (level of love), he has not properly understood the true meaning of *"la ilaha ill-Allah"* or of Tawhid or of *'ubudiyyah* or of loving Allah. There is something lacking in his *iman* and *Tawhid*, and he will suffer pain, regret and anguish accordingly."

Ibn Taymiyah explains that happiness and fulfilment can only be attained by being true slaves of Allah. Feelings of unhappiness, misery and dissatisfaction come from being alienated and far away from Allah, not because of the lack of some of our material needs and wants. Thus the Islamic concept of happiness and fulfilment is diametrically opposed to the materialistic concept, which says that happiness can be achieved through material means. The materialistic view says that mental problems or mental illness is the result of material deprivation, lack of sexual fulfilment, and so on. Islam, on the other hand, says that these problems stem from being away from Allah and ignoring the basic purpose of life, which is to be His true slave.

Happiness and fulfilment, both in this world and the Hereafter, can be achieved only through drawing close to Allah and worshipping Him in the ways prescribed in Islam and demonstrated in the Sunnah of the Prophet ﷺ. Any way other than that of Islam and the Sunnah will only lead to misery, in this world or the next, and on every level from the individual to the social and global.

This book is also evidence that the books of our Islamic *turath* (heritage) and the works of our great scholars have a great deal to say about the human condition. The Revelation came to reform the human soul, and our scholars spoke at length about the human condition in the light of that Divine Revelation. Therefore it does not befit the Muslim to consult or refer to the Western, humanist, psychological tradition, or any other system that is not based on the Qur'an and Sunnah. The translation of this book is intended to enable non-Arabic-speaking Muslims to become further acquainted with their Islamic heritage and to discover the riches left to us by the great scholars.

May Allah guide us to the way of His Messenger ﷺ, and may He enable us to become further acquainted with the words of our scholars regarding the human condition and human psychology. May He enable us to find the way to fulfilment through His Revelation and grant us healing by following the Way He has shown us through His Prophet ﷺ.

Nasiruddin al-Khattab
February 1999

Translator's Notes

Ibn Taymiyah wrote in the style of the great scholars, which differs from the "chapter headings and bullet points" style favoured in the late twentieth century. The scholarly tradition of writing discusses matters in great detail, introducing everything that is connected to the topic, no matter how subtle the connection. Modern readers may find this style rather different to what they are used to, but I have chosen to retain this approach in the translation, as it is more faithful to the original, and builds up an understanding of the main points in a gradual manner that may more easily be retained by the reader. However, in deference to the rushed pace of modern life, sub-headings have been introduced so that readers who prefer to scan the list of contents or dip into different parts of the books may find it readily accessible.

The interpretations of Qur'anic quotations have been taken from the translation by Yusuf Ali's *The Meaning of the Holy Qur'an*. Archaic language has been modernised, e.g. "thou" and "goeth" have been changed to "you" and "goes". Biblical-style language has also been altered, such as changing "servant of Allah" to "slave of Allah", which is closer to the Arabic meaning. Although the word "slave" may sound objectionable to some readers, it is worth noting that it is only by enslavement to Allah that we attain true freedom from worldly bonds.

Arabic symbols used after the names of Prophets and *Sahabah* have the following meanings:

ﷺ *Sall Allahu 'alayhi wa sallam* (may Allah bless him and grant him peace), said after the name of Prophet Muhammad
ﷺ *Radiy Allahu 'anhu* (may Allah be pleased with him), said after the name of one of the Prophet's *Sahabah* (Companions)
ﷺ *Alayhi's-salam* (upon him be peace), said after the name of one of the Prophets

Who is Ibn Taymiyah?

Shaykh al-Islam Taqiy al-Din Abu'l-Abbas Ahmad ibn 'Abd al-Halim ibn 'Abd al-Salam ibn Taymiyah al-Haraani al-Hanbali was born in 1263CE/661AH in Harran, which is now in eastern Turkey, near the border of northern Iraq. He came from a scholarly family and was himself a scholar from an early age, completing his studies whilst still in his teens.

He lived during a time of great upheaval. The Muslim world was being subjected to the attacks of the Tatars from without, and was being torn by sectarianism and innovations from within. He fought on all fronts, military and ideological, to defend pure Islam and the supremacy of the Qur'an and Sunnah. His *jihad* led to him being imprisoned by the authorities who were under the influence of heretical groups, but he continued to write and to speak out even when in jail.

Ibn Taymiyah died in jail in Damascus in 1328CE/728AH. May Allah have mercy on him.

Introduction

Praise be to Allah, we praise Him and seek His help and forgiveness. We seek refuge with Allah from the evil of our own selves and from our evil deeds. Whomsoever Allah guides can never be lead astray, and whomsoever Allah leaves astray cannot be guided.

I bear witness that there is no god but Allah alone, with no partner or associate, and I bear witness that Muhammad is His slave and Messenger.

The prominent scholar, defender of the Sunnah and opponent of *bid'ah* (innovation), Shaykh al-Islam Ahmad ibn 'Abd al-Halim ibn Taymiyah, may Allah have mercy on him, was asked about the *ayah*:

"*O mankind! Worship your Lord...*" (al-Baqarah 2:21)

What is worship *('ibadah),* and what are its implications? Does it include all the issues of *deen* (religion) or not? What is the real essence of *'ubudiyyah* (enslavement to Allah)? Is it the highest level of achievement that can be attained in this world or in the Hereafter, or is there something higher? This is the issue that will be explained here.

Al-'Ubudiyyah

Part One

"I have only created jinns and men, that they may serve [worship] Me."

(al-Dhariyat 51:56)

Dimensions of 'Ibadah

'Ibadah (worship) is a word that includes everything that Allah loves and is pleased with, whether it be words or deeds, open or hidden. So *salah* (prayer), *zakat,* fasting, Hajj, speaking truthfully, fulfilling one's trust, treating one's parents with kindness and respect, upholding the ties of kinship, keeping one's promise, enjoining what is good and forbidding what is evil, striving in *jihad* against the *kuffar* and *munafiqin,* being kind to one's neighbours, orphans, the poor, wayfarers, slaves and animals, praying and making supplication *(du'a'),* remembering Allah *(dhikr),* reading Qur'an, and other good deeds, all come under the heading of *'ibadah.*

Similarly, loving Allah and His Messenger, fearing Allah, turning in repentance to Him, being sincere towards Him, patiently accepting His rulings, being thankful for His blessings, being content with His decree, putting one's trust in Him, hoping for His mercy, fearing His punishment, and so on, also come under the heading of worshipping Allah.

'Ibadah (worship of Allah) is the ultimate goal which Allah loves and with which He is pleased. It is the purpose for which He created His creation, as He says in the Qur'an:

> *"I have only created jinns and men, that they may serve [worship] Me."*
> (al–Dhariyat 51:56)

This is the Message with which all the Messengers were sent, as Nuh ﷺ said to his people:

> *"'...Worship Allah! You have no other god but Him...'"* (al–A'raf 7:59)

Hud ﷺ, Salih ﷺ, Shu'ayb ﷺ and other Messengers also conveyed a similar message to their peoples. Allah said:

> *"For We assuredly sent amongst every People a messenger, (with the command):*
> *'Worship Allah, and eschew evil': of the people were some guided, and some on*
> *whom error became inevitable (established)..."* (al–Nahl 16:36)

"Not a messenger did We send before you without this inspiration sent by Us to him: that there is no god but I, therefore worship and serve Me." (al-Anbiya' 21:25)

"Truly, this ummah [religion] of yours is one religion, and I am your Lord, so worship Me (alone)." (al-Anbiya' 21:92)

"O messengers! Enjoy (all) things good and pure, and work righteousness; for I am well-acquainted with (all) that you do. And verily this Brotherhood [ummah; religion] of yours is a single Brotherhood, and I am your Lord and Cherisher: therefore fear Me (and no other)." (al-Mu'minun 22:51-52)

So this *'ibadah* or worship was made a duty on His Messenger until death, as Allah said:
"And worship your Lord until there comes to you the certainty (i.e. death)." (al-Hijr 15:99)

Allah described His angels and Prophets as being those who worship Him:
"To Him belongs whosoever is in the heavens and on earth. And those who are near Him (i.e. the angels) are not too proud to worship Him, nor are they weary (of His worship)." (al-Anbiya' 21:19)

"Surely, those who are with your Lord (angels) are never too proud to perform acts of worship to Him, but they glorify His praise and prostrate before Him." (al-A'raf 7:206)

Allah condemned those who are too arrogant to worship Him:
"And your Lord says: 'Call on Me; I will answer your (prayer): but those who are too arrogant to worship Me will surely find themselves in Hell - in humiliation!'" (Ghafir 40:60)

Allah described His creation as being in a state of servitude and enslavement to Him *('ubudiyyah)*:

"A spring wherefrom the slaves of Allah will drink, causing it to gush forth abundantly." (al–Insan 76:6)

"And the slaves of (Allah) Most Gracious are those who walk on the earth with humility, and when the ignorant address them, they say, 'Peace!' Those who spend the night in adoration of their Lord prostrate and standing; Those who say: 'Our Lord! Avert from us the wrath of Hell, for its Wrath is indeed an affliction grievous – Evil indeed is it as an abode, and as a place to rest in'; Those who, when they spend, are not extravagant and not niggardly, but hold a just (balance) between those (extremes); Those who invoke not, with Allah, any other god, nor slay such life as Allah has made sacred, except for just cause, nor commit fornication - and any that does this (not only) meets punishment (But) the Penalty on the Day of Judgement will be doubled to him, and he will dwell therein in ignominy – Unless he repents, believes and works righteous deeds. For Allah will change the evil of such persons into good, and Allah is Oft-Forgiving, Most Merciful. And whoever repents and does good has truly turned to Allah with an (acceptable) conversion – Those who witness no falsehood and, if they pass by futility, they pass it by with honourable (avoidance); Those who, when they are admonished with the Signs of their Lord, droop not down at them as if they were deaf or blind; And those who pray, 'Our Lord! Grant unto us wives and offspring who will be the comfort of our eyes, and give us (the grace) to lead the righteous.' Those are the ones who will be rewarded with the highest place in heaven, because of their patient constancy: therein shall they be met with salutations and peace, Dwelling therein - how beautiful an abode and place of rest! Say (to the Rejecters): 'My Lord is not uneasy because of you if you call not on Him: but you have indeed rejected (Him), and soon will come the inevitable (punishment)!'" (al–Furqan 25:63-77)

When Shaytan said: *"'O my Lord! Because You have put me in the wrong, I will make (wrong) fair-seeming to them on the earth, and I will put them all in the wrong - except Your servants among them, sincere and purified (by Your grace)'"* (al–Hijr 15:39-40), Allah said: *"'...over My slaves no authority shall you have, except such as put themselves in the wrong and follow you'"* (al–Hijr 15:42).

Allah described the angels as worshipping Him:

> *"And they say: 'The Most Beneficent (Allah) has begotten a son (or children).'*
> *Glory to Him! They [those whom they call children of Allah, i.e. the angels,*
> *'Isa (Jesus), etc.] are but honoured slaves. They speak not until He has spoken,*
> *and they act on His command. He knows what is before them, and what*
> *is behind them, and they cannot intercede except for him with whom He is*
> *pleased. And they stand in awe for fear of Him."* (al-Anbiya' 21:26–28)

> *"They say: 'The Most Beneficent (Allah) has begotten a son (or children).'*
> *Indeed, you have brought forth (said) a terrible evil thing, whereby the heavens*
> *are almost torn, and the earth split asunder, and the mountains fall in ruins,*
> *that they ascribe a son (or children) to the Most Beneficent (Allah). But it is not*
> *suitable for (the Majesty of) the Most Beneficent that He should beget a son (or*
> *children). There is none in the heavens and the earth but comes unto the Most*
> *Beneficent as a slave. Verily, He knows each one of them, and has counted*
> *them a full counting. And every one of them will come to Him alone on the*
> *Day of Resurrection (without any helper, or protector or defender)."*
> (Maryam 19:88–95)

Prophets are also slaves

Concerning the Messiah, whom some claim was divine as well as being
a Prophet, Allah says:

> *"He was not more than a slave. We granted Our Favour to him, and We made*
> *him an example to the Children of Israel (i.e. his creation without a father)."*
> (al-Zukhruf 43:59)

For this reason the Prophet ﷺ said, according to a *sahih hadith*:

> "Do not exaggerate in praising me the way the Christians do about 'Isa
> ibn Maryam. I am no more than a slave." The *Sahabah* said: "The slave
> of Allah and His messenger." *(Al-Bukhari)*

Even in the context of describing the immense honours bestowed upon the Prophet ﷺ, Allah describes him as a slave. Concerning the *Isra'* (the Prophet's Night Journey), He said:

> *"Glorified (and Exalted) be He (Allah) Who took His slave for a journey by night..."* (al-Isra' 17:1)

Concerning the Revelation, He said:

> *"So did (Allah) convey the Inspiration to His slave [Muhammad, through Jibril]."* (al-Najm 53:10)

Describing the Prophet ﷺ calling upon Him, He said:

> *"Yet when the slave of Allah stands forth to invoke him, they just make around him a dense crowd."* (al-Jinn 72:19)

Concerning challenges about the authenticity of the Qur'an, He said:

> *"And if you are in doubt concerning that which We have sent down to our slave (i.e. Muhammad), then produce a surah (chapter) of the like thereof and call your witnesses besides Allah, if you are truthful."* (al-Baqarah 2:23)

'Ibadah – an all-embracing concept

All of religion is included in the concept of *'ibadah*. A *sahih hadith* states that Jibril came to the Prophet ﷺ in the form of a Bedouin and asked him about Islam. He said:

> "Islam is to testify that there is no god except Allah and that Muhammad is the Messenger of Allah, to establish prayer, to pay *zakat*, to fast in Ramadan, and to make the Pilgrimage to the House (i.e. the Ka'bah) if one is able to." He asked: "And what is *iman* (faith)?" He said: "To believe in Allah, His angels, His Books, His Messengers, and resurrection after death; to believe in divine preordination, both good and bad." He asked: "And what is *ihsan*?" He said: "It is to worship Allah as if you are seeing Him, and although you do not see Him. He sees you." At

the end of the *hadith*, the Prophet ﷺ told his Companions: "That was Jibril, who came to teach you your religion." *(Muslim)*

All of these things are part of religion *(deen)*. The word *deen* (religion) carries the meaning of submission, which means worshipping and obeying Allah, and being humble towards Him. This is the religion of Allah (i.e. Islam).

The root of the word *'ibadah* also carries the meaning of submission and humility. In Arabic a road may be described as *tariq mu'abbad*, i.e. it is smooth and easy for people to walk on.

But the kind of worship that we are commanded to carry out includes both humility and love. It combines the utmost humility to Him with the utmost love for Him.

Degrees of love

The highest degree of love is *tatayyum* (total enthralment). The lowest degree is *'alaqah* (attachment), when the heart is attached to the beloved; then comes *sababah* (infatuation), when the heart is poured out; then *gharam* (passion), when love never leaves the heart; then *'ashaq* (ardent love), and finally *tatayyum*. When we say that a person is enthralled, as it were, by Allah, it means that he worships Allah, because enthralment is like enslavement to the beloved.

When a person submits to another even though he dislikes him, this is not worship or enslavement; when he loves someone but is not subservient to him, as a man might love his child or his friend, this is not worship or enslavement either. Either of them alone is not enough when it comes to worshipping Allah. Allah must be dearer than anything else to the slave; Allah must be more important than all else. Nothing is deserving of complete love and submission except Allah. Love for anything other than Allah is corrupt love, and veneration of anything except Allah is false veneration. Allah says:

"Say: If it be that your fathers, your sons, your brothers, your mates, or your kindred; the wealth that you have gained; the commerce in which you fear a decline; or the dwellings in which you delight - are dearer to you than Allah, or His Messenger, or the striving in His cause - then wait until Allah brings about His Decision..." (al-Tawbah 9:24)

Only for Allah

Love, like obedience, should be only for Allah and His Messenger, and for the sake of earning Allah's pleasure:

"...But it is more fitting that they should please Allah and His Messenger..." (al-Tawbah 9:62)

It is also for Allah and His Messenger to give:

"If only they had been content with what Allah and His Messenger gave them..." (al-Tawbah 9:59)

Worship *('ibadah)* and the things that are connected to it - such as complete trust and fear, and so on - can only be for Allah alone, as He says:

"Say (O Muhammad): 'O People of the Book (Jews and Christians): Come to a word that is just between us and you, that we worship none but Allah, and that we associate no partners with Him, and that none of us shall take others as lords besides Allah.' Then if they turn away, say: 'Bear witness that we are Muslims.'" (Al 'Imran 3:64)

"If only they had been content with what Allah and His Messenger gave them, and had said: 'Sufficient unto us is Allah! Allah and His Messenger will soon give us of His bounty: to Allah do we turn our hopes!' (That would have been the right course)." (al-Tawbah 9:59)

So it is for Allah and His Messenger to give, as He said:

"...So take what the Messenger assigns to you, and deny yourselves that which he withholds from you." (al-Hashr 59:7)

Allah is Sufficient for us

It is only Allah Who is Sufficient for us, as He says:

"Those (i.e. believers) unto whom the people (hypocrites) said: 'Verily, the people (pagans) have gathered against you (a great army), therefore fear them.' But it (only) increased them in Faith, and they said: 'Allah (Alone) is Sufficient for us, and He is the Best Disposer of affairs (for us).'" (Al 'lmran 3:173)

"O Prophet! Allah is Sufficient for you and for the believers who follow you." (al-Anfal 8:64)

The last *ayah* means, "Sufficient for you and those who follow you of the believers, is Allah." Anyone who thinks that it means "Allah and the believers with Him are sufficient for you" is making a grave mistake. Allah also says:

"Is not Allah Sufficient for His slave?..." (al-Zumar 39:36)

In conclusion, therefore, we may say that "slave" *('abd)* means the one who is enslaved by Allah and who submits and humbles himself to Him.

We are all slaves

By this token, all of mankind – whether they are righteous or corrupt, believers or disbelievers, destined for Paradise or for Hell – are slaves of Allah. He is their Lord and Master, their Owner, and they never operate outside of His will and decree. No one, righteous or corrupt, can overstep the limits of His perfect decree. Whatever He wills happens, even if they do not want it to. Whatever they want, if He does not will it, will not happen, as Allah says:

> *"Do they seek other than the Religion of Allah? - while all creatures in the heavens and on earth have, willing or unwilling, bowed to His Will (accepted Islam), and to Him shall they all be brought back."* (Al 'Imran 3:83)

Allah, may He be glorified and exalted, is the Lord of the Worlds, the Creator and Sustainer, the One Who gives life and death, the One Who controls their hearts, the One Who runs their affairs. They have no other lord except Him, whether they recognise this or deny it, whether they are aware of this or are ignorant. But the believers among them recognise this, and believe it, unlike those who are ignorant of it or wilfully deny it out of stubborn pride, which makes them refuse to acknowledge Him or submit to Him, even though they know that Allah is their Lord and Creator. Knowing the truth but being too proud to accept it, is a kind of punishment, as Allah says:

> *"And they rejected those Signs in iniquity and arrogance, though their souls were convinced thereof: so see what was the end of those who acted corruptly!"* (al-Naml 27:14)

> *"The People of the Book know this as they know their own sons; but some of them conceal the truth which they themselves know."* (al-Baqarah 2:146)

> *"...it is not you they reject: it is the Signs of Allah which the wicked condemn."* (al-An'am 6:33)

Lesser kinds of *'ubudiyyah*

When the slave recognises that Allah is his Lord and Creator, and that he is in need of Him, he acknowledges the kind of *'ubudiyyah* or enslavement that has to do with the Lordship *(rububiyyah)* of Allah. So this slave may ask Allah and beseech Him, putting his trust in Him, but at the same time he may be obedient to His commands or disobedient, he may worship Him or he may worship idols and the *Shaytan*. This kind of *'ubudiyyah* is not the factor that marks the difference between the people of Paradise and the people of Hell, nor does it make a man a believer, as Allah says:

> *"Most of them do not believe in Allah without associating (others as partners) with Him!"* (Yusuf 12:106)

Even the *mushrikun* (polytheists, pagans) used to acknowledge that Allah was their Creator, but they used to worship other gods besides Him. Allah said:

> *"If indeed you ask them who it is that created the heavens and the earth, they would be sure to say: 'Allah'..."* (al-Zumar 39:38)

> *"Say: 'To whom belong the earth and all beings therein? (Say) if you know!' They will say: 'To Allah!' Say: 'Yet will you not receive admonition?' Say: 'Who is the Lord of the seven heavens and the Lord of the Throne (of Glory) Supreme?' They will say: '(They belong) to Allah.' Say: 'Will you not then be filled with awe?' Say: 'Who is it in whose hands is the governance of all things - who protects all, but is not protected (of any)? (Say) if you know.' They will say: '(It belongs to Allah).' Say: 'Then how are you deluded?'"* (al-Mu'minun 23:85-89)

Many of those who speak and recognise "reality" (the fact that Allah is the Creator) only bear witness to this fact, which is the cosmic reality *(al-haqiqah al-kawniyyah)* shared by believers and disbelievers, righteous and wrongdoers, alike. Even Iblis and the people of Hell acknowledge this reality. The Qur'an tells us:

> *"(Iblis) said: 'O my Lord! Give me then respite until the Day the (dead) are raised.'"* (Sad 38:79)

> *"(Iblis) said: 'O my Lord! Because You have put me in the wrong, I will make (wrong) fair-seeming to them on the earth, and I will put them all in the wrong.'"* (al-Hijr 15:39)

"(Iblis) said: 'Then, by Your Power, I will put them all in the wrong...'"
(Sad 38:82)

"(Iblis) said: 'Do You see? This is the one whom You have honoured above me! If You will but respite me to the Day of Judgement, I will surely bring his descendants under my sway all but a few!'" (al-Isra' 17:62)

These examples illustrate how Iblis acknowledges that Allah is his Lord and Creator, and the Creator of others. Similarly, the people of Hell will say:

"'Our Lord! Our misfortune overwhelmed us, and we became a people astray!'"
(al-Mu'minun 23:106)

And Allah says concerning them:

"If you could but see when they are confronted with their Lord! He will say, 'Is not this the truth?' They will say, 'Yes, by our Lord!'..." (al-An'am 6:30)

Heeding the commands of Allah is essential

Whoever stops at this point, and does not pay attention to the commands of Allah that constitute part of the "religious reality" *(al-haqiqah al-diniyyah),* which has to do with worshipping Allah as *ilah* (divine) and obeying the commands of Allah and His Messenger – such people are of the same type as Iblis and the people of Hell.

If, in spite of this, a person believes that he is one of the special kind of *awliya'* or one of the people of advanced knowledge who are somehow exempt from having to heed the commands and prohibitions of Islam, then he is one of the worst types of *kafir* and heretic.

Some people think that al-Khidr and others were also exempt from having to obey Allah's commands, because they recognised and acknowledged the will of Allah, but this is one of the worst things that was said by those who disbelieved in Allah and His Messenger, unless they voluntarily become the second type of *'abd,* which means slave in the sense of worshipper *('abid).* So the slave worships Allah and does not worship anything or anyone else; he obeys the commands of Allah and His Messenger; he supports the believing friends *(awliya')* of Allah and opposes those who fight them.

True worship

This kind of worship has to do with the divine nature of Allah *(uluhiyyah),* which is why the slogan of *Tawhid* is *"La ilaha ill-Allah".* This is in contrast to those who acknowledge the lordship of Allah but do not worship Him, or worship other gods alongside Him.

The word *"ilah"* (usually translated as "god") refers to something or someone that the heart loves and is attached to with the utmost love, veneration, respect, honour, fear and hope, and so on.

This kind of worship is that which Allah loves and is pleased with. It is the characteristic which He describes in His chosen slaves, and it is the message with which He sent His Messengers.

The slave *('abd)* is the one who is enslaved, whether he recognises that or denies it; this applies to both the believer and the disbeliever.

Worship and enslavement

The difference between the worshipper *('abid)* and the one who is enslaved *(mu'abbad)* is the difference between the religious realities which have to do with the worship of Allah and the religion and commandments which

He loves and with which He is pleased, and for which He will honour people with Paradise, and the cosmic realities which are common to believers and disbelievers, righteous and corrupt. Whoever stops at the point of the cosmic realities and does not follow the religious realities is a follower of the accursed Iblis, one of those who disbelieve in the Lord of the Worlds. The same applies to one who accepts only some of the religious realities but not others. His faith and loyalty to Allah will be lacking in as much as his acceptance of the religious realities is lacking. This is a serious issue, in which many have erred and in which many of those who wish to draw close to Allah have become confused. Even some of the greatest *shaykhs,* who claim to understand these realities, to believe in *Tawhid* and to have knowledge, have made this mistake – in fact so many of them that only Allah knows their true number.

Al-qada' wa'l-qadar (Divine decree and preordainment)

Shaykh 'Abd al-Qadir, may Allah have mercy on him, referred to this, and explained that when it comes to matters of *al-qada' wa'l-qadar* (divine decree and preordainment), many people would not even touch the topic, "but a small window has been opened for me on this issue, and I sought to deal with the decree of Allah with the help of Allah for the sake of Allah. The real man is the one who faces up to the decree of Allah, not the one who meekly submits and gives in to it."

What the *shaykh* was describing here is what Allah and His Messenger commanded, but many people erred on this matter. They may recognise that divine decree may cause one of them, or anyone else, to be disobedient and commit sins, even to commit *kufr,* and that this is happening by the will and decree of Allah, under His lordly rule, so they think that meekly submitting to this and accepting it is the essence of religion and worship. So they may say something similar to what the *mushrikin* said:

"... 'If Allah had wished, we should not have given partners to Him, nor should we have had any taboos.'..." (al-An'am 6:148)

"... 'Shall we then feed those whom, if Allah had so willed, He would have fed (Himself)?...'" (Ya-Sin 36:47)

"... 'If it had been the Will of (Allah) Most Gracious, we should not have worshipped such (deities)!'..." (al-Zukhruf 43:20)

If they had been truly guided, they would have known that it is up to us to accept Allah's decree and to face any calamities – such as poverty, sickness and fear – that may befall us as a result with patience. Allah says:

"No kind of calamity can occur, except by the leave of Allah: and if anyone believes in Allah, (Allah) guides his heart (aright)..." (al-Taghabun 64:11)

Some of the *salaf* said: This refers to a man who is stricken by some calamity, but he knows that it is from Allah, so he accepts it and submits to it. Allah said:

"No misfortune can happen on earth or in your souls but is recorded in a decree before We bring it into existence: that is truly easy for Allah: in order that you may not despair over matters that pass you by, nor exult over favours bestowed upon you..." (al-Hadid 57:22-23)

The Prophets and the Divine Decree

Al-Bukhari and Muslim reported that the Prophet ﷺ said:

"Adam and Musa engaged in a debate. Musa said: 'You are Adam whom Allah created with His own hand, and breathed into you of His spirit; He made His angels prostrate to you and taught you the names of all things. So why did you cause yourself and us to be expelled from Paradise?' Adam said: 'You are Musa, whom Allah chose to convey His

Message and spoke directly with you. Do you not realise that this was decreed for me before I was even created?'"

Adam 🖎 did not use the idea of *qadar* as an excuse in his discussion with Musa 🖎, or think that a sinner can use this as an excuse for sin. No intelligent Muslim would say such a thing. If *qadar* really was an excuse, then it would have been an excuse for Iblis, or for the peoples of Nuh 🖎 and Hud 🖎, and for every *kafir*. Neither did Musa 🖎 mean to blame Adam 🖎 for his sin, because Adam 🖎 repented to his Lord, and was forgiven and guided, but he was taking him to task for the calamity that befell mankind as a result of his error. This is why he asked, "Why did you cause yourself and us to be expelled from Paradise?" and Adam 🖎 answered, "This was decreed for me before I was even created."

Both the deed and its consequences were decreed by Allah. Whatever calamities are decreed should be submitted to, because this means complete acceptance of Allah as *Rabb* (Lord).

The case of sin

But when it comes to sin, the slave should not commit sins. If he does commit sin, then he must repent and seek forgiveness. So he repents for all kinds of shortcomings, and bears calamities with patience. Allah says:

"So be patient. Verily the promise of Allah is true, and ask forgiveness for your fault..." (Ghafir 40:55)

"...But if you remain patient and become al-muttaqun (the pious), not the least harm will their cunning do to you..." (Al 'Imran 3:120)

"...but if you persevere patiently, and become al-muttaqun (the pious), then verily, that will be a determining factor in all affairs." (Al 'Imran 3:186)

"[Yusuf said]: 'Verily, he who fears Allah with obedience to Him, and is patient, then surely Allah causes not the reward of the muhsinun (good-doers) to be lost.'" (Yusuf 12:90)

Al-'Ubudiyyah

Part Two

"You will not find any people who believe in Allah and the Last Day, loving those who resist Allah and His Messenger, even though they were their fathers or their sons, or their brothers or their kindred. For such He has written Faith in their hearts, and strengthened them with a spirit from Himself..."

(al–Mujadilah 58:22)

The obligation of enjoining the good

When it comes to people's sins, the slave is obliged to enjoin what is good and forbid what is evil, as much as he is able to. So he should strive in *jihad* against the *kuffar* and *munafiqin*, and support the friends of Allah and oppose His enemies, loving and hating for the sake of Allah, as Allah says:

"O you who believe! Take not My enemies and yours as friends (or protectors) - offering them (your) love, even though they have rejected the Truth that has come to you, and have (on the contrary) driven out the Messenger and yourselves (from your homes), (simply) because you believe in Allah your Lord! If you have come out to strive in My Way and to seek My Good Pleasure, (take them not as friends), holding secret converse of love (and friendship) with them: for I know full well all that you conceal and all that you reveal. And any of you that does this has strayed from the Straight Path. If they were to get the better of you, they would behave to you as enemies, and stretch forth their hands and their tongues against you for evil; and they desire that you should reject the Truth. Of no profit to you will be your relatives and your children on the Day of Judgement: He will judge between you: for Allah sees well all that you do. There is for you an excellent example (to follow) in Ibrahim and those with him, when they said to their people: 'We are clear of you and of whatever you worship besides Allah: we have rejected you, and there has arisen, between us and you, enmity and hatred forever - unless you believe in Allah and Him alone.'..." (al-Mumtahinah 60:1-4)

"You will not find any people who believe in Allah and the Last Day, loving those who resist Allah and His Messenger, even though they were their fathers or their sons, or their brothers or their kindred. For such He has written Faith in their hearts, and strengthened them with a spirit from Himself..." (al-Mujadilah 58:22)

"Shall We then treat the (submitting) Muslims like the mujrimun (criminals, polytheists, disbelievers, etc.)?" (al-Qalam 68:35)

"Shall We treat those who believe and work deeds of righteousness, the same as those who do mischief on earth? Shall we treat those who guard against evil, the same as those who turn aside from the right?" (Sad 38:28)

"What! Do those who seek after evil ways think that We shall hold them equal with those who believe and do righteous deeds - that equal will be their life and their death? Ill is the judgment that they make." (al-Jathiyah 45:21)

"The blind and the seeing are not alike; Nor are the depth of Darkness and the Light; Nor are the (chilly) shade and the (genial) heat of the sun: Nor are alike those that are living and those that are dead..." (Fatir 35:19-22)

"Allah puts forward a Parable - a man belonging to many partners at variance with each other, and a man belonging entirely to one master: are these two equal in comparison?..." (al-Zumar 39:29)

"Allah sets forth the Parable (of two men: one) a slave under the dominion of another; he has no power of any sort; and (the other) a man on whom We have bestowed goodly favours from Ourselves. And he spends thereof (freely), privately and publicly: are the two equal? (By no means;) Praise be to Allah. But most of them understand not. Allah sets forth (another) Parable of two men: one of them dumb, with no power of any sort: a wearisome burden is he to his master; whichever way he directs him, he brings no good: is such a man equal with one who commands justice, and is on a Straight Way?" (al-Nahl 16:75-76)

"Not equal are the dwellers of the Fire and the dwellers of Paradise. It is the dwellers of Paradise that will be successful." (al-Hashr 59:20)

Thus does Allah distinguish between the people of Truth and the people of falsehood, between the obedient and the disobedient, between the righteous and the sinful, between those who are guided and those who have gone astray, between those who speak the truth and those who lie.

No equality

Whoever recognises only the cosmic reality *(al-haqiqah al-kawniyyah)*, whilst ignoring the religious reality *(al-haqiqah al-diniyyah)*, will see all kinds of things as equal where Allah has clearly differentiated between them, to such an extent that he may even regard Allah and idols as equal, as Allah says:

> *"They will say while contending therein [in Hell], By Allah, we were truly in a manifest error, when We held you (false gods) as equals (in worship) with the Lord of the Worlds."* (al-Shu'ara' 26:96–98)

Some even went as far as equating Allah with everything that exists, and saying that the worship and obedience that is due to Allah is also due to everything in existence, because Allah and His creation are the same. This is one of the worst forms of *kufr* and heresy about the Lord of mankind. Their *kufr* reaches such an extent that not only do they not believe that they are slaves of Allah, in either the sense of being enslaved or of being willing worshippers, but they claim that they themselves are Allah, as a number of their evil leaders have claimed in their books, where they say that not only are they worshippers, but they are also the objects of worship.

But this is not reality at all, either cosmic or religious. This is falsehood that demonstrates ignorance of the cosmic reality: how else could they describe the Creator and His creation as being one and the same, or describe every attribute, whether good or bad, as belonging to both the Creator and His creation?

The people of the Qur'an

The believers, on the other hand, leaders and masses alike, are the people of the Qur'an, as the Prophet ﷺ said:

"Allah has families among mankind." He was asked, "Who are they, O Messenger of Allah?" He said, "The people of the Qur'an are the people of Allah, the ones who are closest to Him." *(Ahmad)*

These people, the believers, know that Allah is the Lord, Owner and Creator of all things. The Creator, may He be glorified, is different from His creation. He is not incarnated in it, neither is He one with it. The Christians are regarded as *kuffar* because they believe in the Incarnation and think that Allah is one with the Messiah, especially. What, then, should we say about one who applies this idea to the whole of creation, even though they know that Allah has commanded them to obey Him and His Messenger, and has forbidden them to disobey Him and His Messenger, that He does not like wrongdoing, that He does not want *kufr* for His slaves, and that His creatures should worship Him, obey His commands, and seek His help in all this, as He says in the opening chapter of His Book: *"You (Alone) we worship, and You (Alone) we ask for help"* (al-Fatihah 1:5)?

Striving

One aspect of worshipping and obeying Him is: to enjoin what is good and to forbid what is evil, as much as one can and to strive in *ijtihad* for His sake against *kufr* and hypocrisy. So the believers strive to establish His religion, seeking His help and thus wiping out whatever *sayi'at* (evil deeds) may have been foreordained and repelling whatever consequences may be feared, just as a man may cancel out his present hunger and ward off future hunger by eating, or protect himself from cold in winter by wearing the proper clothing, or seek to protect himself from anything he dislikes. The people asked the Prophet ﷺ, "What do you think of the medicines, recitations and precautions we use (against sickness)? Will they change the decree *(qadar)* of Allah at all?" He said, "They are part of the decree of Allah." In another *hadith*, he said, "*Du'a'* (supplication) and decreed calamities meet and wrestle between heaven and earth" *(Ahmad, Ibn Majah and al-Tirmidhi).*

This is the attitude of those who believe in Allah and His Messenger and worship Allah. This is all part of *'ibadah* (worship).

Iniquitous inconsistencies

Those who acknowledge the cosmic reality – that Allah is Lord and Sustainer of all – but take this as an excuse not to obey the commands of His religion and law, have gone far astray.

The extremists among them even take *qadar* (Allah's decree) as an excuse for all the things they do contrary to the Law of Allah. What they say is even worse than the claims of the Jews and Christians. It is more like the words of the *mushrikin* referred to in the Qur'an:

"... *'If Allah has wished, we should not have given partners to Him, nor should we have had any taboos'...*" (al-An'am 6:148)

"... *'If it had been the Will of (Allah) Most Gracious, we should not have worshipped such (deities)'...*" (al-Zukhruf 43:20)

They are among the most inconsistent people on earth. Indeed, everyone who uses *qadar* as an excuse is inconsistent, because if he does something wrong he blames it on others, but he cannot accept what is done to him by others. If a wrongdoer oppresses him or others, and spreads corruption on earth, and sheds people's blood, and makes adultery and fornication lawful for himself, and destroys crops and cattle, and does other kinds of harm which people cannot endure, then he must resist this type of *qadar* and punish the oppressive wrongdoer by putting a stop to the aggression committed by him and others like him. So it may be said to him: "If *qadar* is an excuse, then let everyone do whatever he wants to you and to others. If *qadar* is not an excuse, then your argument that it is an excuse has no basis."

These people, who use the idea of cosmic reality as an excuse for not following the laws of Allah, do not even adhere consistently to this argument; they just follow their own ideas and whims. As some of the scholars said to them: "When it comes to obeying Allah, you are *Qadari* (i.e. you use *qadar* as an excuse not to obey Him); when it comes to sin you are *Jabari* (i.e. you say that it was decreed and you cannot help it); whatever school of thought happens to agree with the whim of the moment is the one that you follow."

False claims of gnosis

Among them there are those who claim to have the ultimate deep knowledge or gnosis *(tahqiq* and *ma'rifah)* and claim that the duty to obey Allah's commands and heed His prohibitions applies only to those who think that their deeds and attributes come from themselves. But the one who believes that his deeds are not his own because they are created by Allah and he is forced to do them, and that Allah is controlling all his movements as He controls everything else, thinks that he is no longer subject to the commands or prohibitions of Allah, or to the promise of Paradise or threat of Hell.

They say that whoever recognises the will of Allah is no longer subject to the duties (of Islam). They claim that al-Khidr was free of such obligations because he recognised the will of Allah.

They differentiate between the common masses and the "elite" who have recognised the cosmic reality and have acknowledged that Allah is the Creator of the deeds of His slaves and that He is the One Who is possessed of a will and is running the affairs of all beings.

They believe that there is a difference between the one who merely knows this at an abstract level and the one who truly sees and recognises it. So they do not believe that the one who merely knows and believes it should be freed from all obligations; that only applies to the one who truly recognises it and no longer sees his deeds as being his own.

They take the idea of being forced by divine will to do things as a reason not to follow the duties prescribed by Allah. This is a trap into which many of those who claim to have true knowledge and belief in *Tawhid* have fallen.

Confused views of *qadar*

The reason for this is that they could not comprehend the fact that a slave may be instructed to do something when it has been decreed that he will do the opposite, which is a fact that the *Mu'tazilah* and other *Qadari* groups failed to grasp.

The *Mu'tazilah* recognised the commands and prohibitions prescribed by Allah, but they rejected the idea of *al-qada' wa'l-qadar* (the divine decree and foreordainment), which has to do with the general will of Allah and the idea that He is the Creator of the deeds of His slaves. This group recognises the idea of *al-qada' wa'l-qadar,* but they think that the one who reaches the level of recognising *qadar* is no longer subject to the commands and prohibitions of Allah; they could not, however, claim that this freedom from obligation applies to all and sundry.

This idea is worse than the belief of the *Mu'tazilah,* and none of the *salaf* held such a belief. They claim that the commands and prohibitions apply only to those who are blind to the cosmic reality, and that the one who has reached the level of recognising this reality is no longer subject to these commands and prohibitions. They say that such a person has become one of the elite. Perhaps in this way they are misinterpreting the *ayah: "And worship your Lord until there comes unto you the certainty"* (al-Hijr 15:99). To them, "the certainty" *(al-yaqin)* means the knowledge of this reality.

What they say is blatant *kufr,* even though there are those who fall into this error without realising that it is *kufr.* It is an undeniable fact in Islam that the commands and prohibitions apply to every sane person until he dies; he can never be in a position where these rules no longer apply, not by recognising *qadar* or in any other way. Whoever does not recognise this should be told about it and have the facts explained to him, then if he persists in this belief that the commands and prohibitions may no longer apply to some, he should be executed.

These ideas have become widespread among many of the later generations, but they were unknown among the first generations of this *ummah.* These ideas represent a hostile challenge to Allah and His Messenger; they turn people away from His Path, deny His Messengers and oppose His Wisdom, even though the one who follows them may be ignorant of the fact that they are wrong and may believe that he is following the way of the Prophet ﷺ and the true *awliya'* (friends) of Allah. So his position is that of one who believes that prayer is not obligatory for him, because of the emotional status that he thinks he has reached with Allah; or that wine is permitted for him, because he is one of the elite *(khawas)* who cannot be harmed by drinking wine; or that fornication is permitted for him, because he has become like an ocean that cannot be contaminated by sins, and so on!

The *mushrikin's* rejection of the Prophet ﷺ

There is no doubt that the *mushrikin's* rejection of the Prophet ﷺ revolved around two issues: their innovations that contradicted the laws of Allah, and their use of *qadar* as an excuse to go against the commands of Allah.

The type of people we have described above have their counterparts among the *mushrikin*, because either they introduce innovations or they use *qadar* as an excuse, or they do both at once, as Allah said about the *mushrikin*:

"When they do anything that is shameful, they say: 'We found our fathers doing so' and 'Allah commanded us thus'. Say: 'Nay, Allah never commands what is shameful: do you say of Allah what you know not?'" (al-A'raf 7:28)

"Those who give partners (to Allah) will say: 'If Allah had wished, we should not have given partners to Him, nor would our fathers: nor should we have had any taboos'..." (al-An'am 6:148)

The Qur'an also mentions the innovations which the *mushrikin* had introduced, such as allowing things that had been prohibited, and worshipping Allah in ways that He had not prescribed:

"And they say that such and such cattle and crops are taboo, and none should eat of them except those whom - so they say - We wish; further, there are cattle forbidden to yoke or burden, and cattle on which, (at slaughter), the name of Allah is not pronounced..." (al-An'am 6:138)

"O Children of Adam! Let not Shaytan seduce you in the same manner as he got your parents out of the Garden... When they do anything that is shameful, they say: 'We found our fathers doing so': and 'Allah commanded us thus'. Say: 'Nay, Allah never commands what is shameful: do you say of Allah what you know not?' Say: 'My Lord has commanded justice; and that you set your whole selves to Him at every time and place of prayer... ...eat and drink: but waste not by excess, for Allah loves not the wasters.' Say: 'Who has forbidden the beautiful (gifts) of Allah, which He has produced for His slaves, and things, clean and pure, (which He has provided) for sustenance?...' Say: 'The things that my Lord has indeed forbidden are: shameful deeds, whether open or secret; sins and trespasses against truth or reason; assigning of partners to Allah, for which He has given no authority; and saying things about Allah of which you have no knowledge.'" (al-A'raf 7:27-33)

These people may call the innovation they have introduced "reality", just as they call the *qadar* they recognise "reality". But for them reality means the attitude whereby a person is restricted, not by the commands and prohibitions of Allah, but by what he sees and likes and feels in his heart, despite the fact that his heart may be completely heedless of Allah.

Pursuit of whims and desires

But they do not use *qadar* as an excuse all the time. In fact, the basis of their behaviour is the pursuit of their own whims and desires, and their "reality" is what they think and what they like. They tell others to follow their whims instead of telling them to follow the command of Allah and His Messenger. This is similar to the *bid'ah* of the *Jahamiyyah* and other Muslim philosophers *(ahl al-kalam),* who took their invented ideas, which contradicted the Qur'an and Sunnah, as facts based on reason which should be believed in, instead of believing in what was conveyed in sound reports (Qur'an and Sunnah). When it comes to the Qur'an and Sunnah, either they misinterpret them, taking things out of context, or they ignore them completely, neither contemplating nor studying them, but saying, "Allah knows best what this means; we will not try to understand it," whilst at the same time they insist on believing the opposite of what is intended therein.

If you examine the *Jahami* claims about their "facts based on reason" which contradict the Qur'an and Sunnah, you will realise that it is little more than nonsense and corrupt beliefs. Similarly, when you examine what those people claim to have attained of being true *awliya'* (friends) of Allah, in contradiction to the Qur'an and Sunnah, you will find that this is based on the whims and desires followed by those who are the enemies of Allah, not His friends.

Why are people misguided?

The main reason why anyone is misguided is because he gives precedence to his own opinion over the guidance revealed from Allah, and he prefers to follow his own whims rather than the commands of Allah. A person's tastes and emotions depend on his likes and desires.

The people of faith have their own tastes and emotions, as the Prophet ﷺ explained in a *sahih hadith*:

"There are three things, whoever has them has discovered the sweetness of faith: when Allah and His Messenger are more beloved to him than anyone else, when he loves another only for the sake of Allah, and when he would hate to return to *kufr* after Allah has saved him from it just as he would hate to be thrown into fire." *(Al-Bukhari and Muslim)*

"He has tasted the sweetness of faith, who accepts Allah as his Lord, Islam as his religion, and Muhammad as his Prophet." *(Muslim)*

But in the case of the people of *kufr,* innovation and desires, their tastes and emotions are in accordance with their own wants, likes and whims.

Wrong kinds of love

Sufyan ibn 'Uyaynah was asked, "Why do the people of whims love their desires so much?" He said, "Have you forgotten the words of Allah, '...*and their hearts absorbed (the worship) of the calf because of their disbelief...*' (al–Baqarah 2:93)?"

The worshippers of idols love their gods, as Allah said:

"*And of mankind are some who take (for worship) others besides Allah as rivals (to Allah). They love them as they love Allah. But those who believe love Allah more (than anything else)...*" (al–Baqarah 2:165)

"But, if they hearken not to you, know that they only follow their own lusts: and who is more astray than one who follows his own lusts, devoid of guidance from Allah ?..." (al-Qasas 28:50)

"...They follow nothing but conjecture and what their own souls desire! - even though there has already come to them Guidance from their Lord!" (al-Najm 53:23)

These people are easily swayed, and they love to listen to poetry and songs that could provoke all kinds of love, not just the unique kind of love which distinguishes the people of faith. So the love that a person feels, whether it is for Allah, or for idols, or the cross, or their homelands, or their brethren, or young boys, or women, will be stirred up by these poems and songs. These are the people who follow their own inclinations and emotions, with no consideration for the Qur'an and Sunnah, or the way of the first and best generations of this *ummah* (the *salaf*).

The one who goes against the Message with which the Messenger of Allah was sent, which is to worship Allah alone, and to obey Him and His Messenger, can never be a true follower of the religion prescribed by Allah, as Allah says:

"Then We put you on the (right) Way of Religion: so follow that (Way), and follow not the desires of those who know not. They will be of no use to you in the sight of Allah: it is only wrongdoers (that stand as) protectors, one to another: but Allah is the Protector of the Righteous." (al-Jathiyah 45:18-19)

Indeed, they are following their own desires, not the guidance of Allah, as He says:

"Or have they partners with Allah (false gods), who have instituted for them a religion which Allah has not allowed?..." (al-Shura 42:21)

Sometimes they indulge in a form of *bid'ah* which they call *"haqiqah"* (reality), and give it precedence over the religion which Allah has prescribed; sometimes they use the universal/cosmic reality as an excuse not to pay heed to true religion, as in the case of the *mushrikin* described in the Qur'anic *ayat* quoted above.

Among them there is a group whom they hold in the highest esteem. These people adhere to whatever takes their fancy of the obligatory duties or prohibitions of religion, but they are misguided because they ignore some of the prescribed ways of worship, thinking that when a person reaches the status of *arif* by acknowledging *qadar,* all this no longer applies to him. For example, they may think that *tawakkul* (putting one's trust in Allah) and *du'a',* etc., are only for the general masses, not for the elite, on the basis that the one who recognises *qadar* would realise that whatever is decreed is going to happen, so he does not need to do any of these things. This is clear and manifest error.

Destiny

Allah has decreed that things will happen for certain reasons (cause and effect), so a person's ultimate happiness (in Paradise) or misery (in Hell) depends on the appropriate causes, as the Prophet 鄴 said:

> "Allah has created for Paradise its people, and has created it for them, whilst they are still in the loins of their fathers, so they will do the deeds of the people of Paradise. And He has created for Hell its people, and has created it for them, whilst they are still in the loins of their fathers, so they will do the deeds of the people of Hell." *(Ahmad, Muslim and Abu Dawud)*

When the Prophet 鄴 told the people that Allah has written all the destinies, they asked, "O Messenger of Allah! Should we give up striving and leave it all to our destiny?" He said, "No, keep striving, because whatever a person is created for will be made easy for him. If he is one of the people of happiness (Paradise), it will be easy for him to do the deeds of the people of happiness, and if he is one of the people of misery (Hell), it will be easy for him to do the deeds of the people of misery" *(Al-Bukhari and Muslim).*

Tests and *tawakkul*

Everything that Allah commands His slaves to do as the means to an end *(asbab)* is a form of worship, and *tawakkul* (putting one's trust in Allah) is always associated with worship, as Allah says:

> *"...Then worship Him and put your trust in Him..."* (Hud 11:123)

> *"...Say: 'He is my Lord! There is no god but He! On Him is my trust and to Him do I turn!'"* (al-Ra'd 13:30)

> *"[Shu'ayb said:] '...In Him I trust and unto Him I look.'"* (Hud 11:88)

Among them there is another group who ignore *mustahabb* (recommended) deeds but will do those which are *wajib* (obligatory), and so their status decreases accordingly.

Another group is tested by means of the extraordinary events and miracles that happen to them, such as telling about the unseen, or having their *du'a's* answered in a remarkable fashion, and so on. In this way, these people may be distracted from the duties of *'ibadah,* gratitude, etc. that they have been commanded to do. These extraordinary events often happen in order to distract those who are striving to discipline themselves, but one can be saved from this by always adhering to the commands of Allah, with which He sent His Messenger, as al-Zuhri said, "Those who passed away before us of the *salaf* used to say: 'Adherence to the Sunnah is salvation.'" This is because the Sunnah, as Malik (may

Allah have mercy on him) said, is like Noah's Ark: whoever boards it
will be saved, and whoever stays behind will be doomed.

'Ibadah, righteousness and Tawhid

'Ibadah (worship), obedience, righteousness and following the straight
path all refer to one thing, which may be summed up in the following
two points:
1. That one does not worship anyone or anything except Allah.
2. That one does not worship Him in any way except the way that He
   Himself has prescribed, and that one does not worship Him according to
   one's own whims and desires or follow *bid'ah* (innovations) in worship.

Allah says:

> "...whoever expects to meet his Lord, let him work righteousness, and in the
> worship of his Lord, admit no one as partner." (al-Kahf 18:110)

> "Nay - whoever submits his whole self to Allah and is a doer of good - he will
> get his reward with his Lord: on such shall be no fear, nor shall they grieve."
> (al-Baqarah 2:112)

> "Who can be better in religion than one who submits his whole self to Allah,
> does good, and follows the way of Ibrahim the true in faith? For Allah did take
> Ibrahim for a friend." (al-Nisa' 4:124)

Righteous deeds *(al-'aml al-salih)* means excellence and perfection, and
doing good deeds *(al-hasanat)*. Good deeds *(al-hasanat)* means that which
Allah and His Messenger love, which is what they have commanded,
whether it is *wajib* or *mustahabb*.

Any innovation in religion that is not found in the Qur'an or in the *sahih*
texts of the Sunnah is not a part of Islam - no matter who is suggesting

it or doing it. Allah does not love such innovations and neither does His Messenger, so it cannot be counted as a righteous deed or a good deed, just as actions that are not permitted – such as immorality or wrongdoing or oppression – cannot be counted as righteous deeds or good deeds.

Sincerity towards Allah

The Qur'anic phrases: *"...and in the worship of his Lord, admit no one as partner"* (al-Kahf 18:110) and *"...one who submits his whole self to Allah..."* (al-Nisa' 4:124), refer to sincerity in religion and submission to Allah alone. 'Umar ibn al-Khattab ⬥ used to say, "O Allah, make all my deeds righteous and make them sincerely for Your sake, and let not anyone else have a share in them (i.e. in the intention)."

Al-Fudayl ibn 'Ayyad said, concerning the *ayah "...that He may try which of you is best in deed"* (al-Mulk 67:2): "[It means which of you is] most sincere and most correct." They asked him, "O Abu 'Ali, what do you mean?" He said, "If the deed is sincere but is not correct, it is not acceptable. If the deed is correct but is not sincere, it is not acceptable either. [It is not acceptable] unless it is both sincere and correct. Sincerity means that it should be only for Allah, and correctness means that it should be in accordance with the Sunnah."

Worship plus

It might be asked: if all that Allah loves is included under the heading of *'ibadah,* then why did He add other things to the idea of worship? For example, He says:

"You do we worship, and Your help we seek." (al-Fatihah 1:5)

"...then worship Him and put your trust in Him..." (Hud 11:123)

"That you should worship Allah, fear Him, and obey me [His Messenger, Nuh]." (Nuh 71:3)

The answer is that there are similar instances elsewhere in the Qur'an, for example, when Allah says: *"...for Prayer restrains from shameful and unjust deeds..."* (al-'Ankabut 29:45); shameful deeds *(al-fahsha')* are one kind of unjust deeds *(al-munkar)*, and would be included under this heading. Similarly, Allah says: *"Allah commands justice, the doing of good, and liberality to kith and kin, and He forbids all shameful deeds, and injustice and rebellion..."* (al-Nahl 16:90). Liberality to kith and kin is part of justice and the doing of good *(al-'adl wa'l-ihsan)*, just as shameful deeds and rebellion are part of injustice *(al-munkar)*. And Allah says: *"As to those who hold fast to the Book and establish regular Prayer..."* (al-A'raf 7:170); establishing regular prayer is an important part of holding fast to the Book.

Similarly, Allah says of His Prophets: *"...These were ever quick in emulation in good works; they used to call on Us with love and reverence..."* (al-Anbiya' 21:90). Their calling on Allah with love and reverence was part of their good works. There are many other examples in the Qur'an where a thing that appears to be added is in fact part of what has already been referred to.

This adding of ideas is sometimes used where one of them is part of the other, but is added to draw particular attention to it, because there is a need to mention it in both general and specific terms. At other times, it may be the case that the same word could indicate different meanings when it is mentioned alone and when it is mentioned in conjunction with other things, so when it is mentioned alone it has a general meaning, and when it is mentioned in conjunction with something else, it has a specific meaning. An example may be seen in the words *faqir* and *miskin*. When each is mentioned alone, the meanings are interchangeable, as in the *ayat "...those in need [fuqara', pl. of faqir], who, in Allah's cause, are restricted (from travel)..."* (al-Baqarah 2:273) and *"...feed ten indigent persons [masakin, pl. of miskin]..."* (al–Ma'idah 5:89). But when the *words faqir* and *miskin* appear together, as in the *ayah "Alms are for the poor [fuqara']* *and the needy [masakin]..."* (al–Tawbah 9:60), they refer to two different kinds of people.

It was said that when the specific is mentioned after the general, it is not included in the meaning of the general, rather it is like the cases referred to above.

In fact, this is not necessarily always the case. Allah says:

"Whoever is an enemy to Allah, and His angels and prophets, to Jibril and Mika'il..." (al–Baqarah 2:98)

"And remember We took from the Prophets their Covenant: as (We did) from you: from Nuh, Ibrahim, Musa, and 'Isa the son of Maryam..." (al–Ahzab 33:7)

The specific may be mentioned alongside the general for various reasons, sometimes because it has a special meaning which is not included in the general term, as is the case with Nuh ﷺ, Ibrahim ﷺ, Musa ﷺ and 'Isa ﷺ, and sometimes because the general term may refer to something abstract, and its meaning is not clear, as in the *ayah "...a guidance to those who are al-muttaqun (pious), who believe in the ghayb (unseen) and perform al-salah (prayer), and spend out of what We have provided for them, and who believe in that which has been sent down (revealed) to you (O Muhammad) and in that which was sent down before you..."* (al–Baqarah 2:2-4).

The phrase *"believe in the ghayb (unseen)"* refers to every type of unseen which we are required to believe in, but this is a very abstract and general term, in which there is nothing to indicate that *"that which has been sent down (revealed) to you (O Muhammad) and that which was sent down before you"* is part of the *ghayb* (unseen).

Similarly, Allah says:

> *"Recite what is sent of the Book by inspiration to you, and establish regular Prayer..."* (al-'Ankabut 29:45)

> *"As to those who hold fast by the Book and establish regular Prayer..."* (al-A'raf 7:170)

Tilawah (translated here as "reciting") means acting in accordance with the Book, as Ibn Mas'ud said concerning the *ayah* *"Those to whom We have sent the Book study it as it should be studied..."* (al-Baqarah 2:121). He said, "They accept what it permits and heed what it prohibits. They believe in those *ayat* whose meaning is not clear and well-established, and they act in accordance with those *ayat* whose meaning is clear and well-established."

Following the Book includes *salah* (prayer) and other things, but prayer is mentioned specifically because of its special status. As Allah said to Musa ﷺ: *"Verily, I am Allah: there is no god but I: so worship Me (only), and establish regular prayer for celebrating My praise"* (Ta-Ha 20:14). Establishing prayer for celebrating His praise (or remembering Him: *dhikr)* is one of the best forms of worship. Similarly, Allah says:

> *"...Keep your duty to Allah and fear Him, and speak (always) the truth."* (al-Ahzab 33:71)

> *"Do your duty to Allah and fear Him. Seek the means of approach to Him..."* (al-Ma'idah 5:35)

> *"Fear Allah and be with those who are true (in word and deed)."* (al-Tawbah 9:119)

All of these things form a part of the *taqwa* (fear of Allah) which is referred to in these *ayat*. Similarly, Allah says:

> *"...Then worship Him and put your trust in Him..."* (Hud 11:123)

Putting one's trust in Him (*tawakkul*) means seeking His help, which is also a part of worshipping Allah, but it is mentioned specifically in order to draw attention to it. Prayer is the means to all other forms of worship, because Allah cannot be worshipped except with His help.

'Ubudiyyah: the route to perfection

Man can only attain perfection by being a true slave of Allah. The more his servitude ('*ubudiyyah*) increases, the more perfect he becomes and the higher he rises in status. Whoever imagines that a person could release himself from this servitude in some way or another, or that releasing oneself from it is better and more perfect, is one of the most ignorant of people and one of the furthest astray. Allah says:

"And they say: '(Allah) Most Gracious has begotten offspring.' Glory to Him! They are (but) servants raised to honour. They speak not before He speaks, and they act (in all things) by His command. He knows what is before them, and what is behind them, and they offer no intercession except for those who are acceptable, and they stand in awe and reverence of His (Glory)."
(al-Anbiya' 21:26-28)

"They say: '(Allah) Most Gracious has begotten a son!' Indeed you have put forth a thing most monstrous! As if the skies are ready to burst, the earth to split asunder, and the mountains to fall down in utter ruin, That they should invoke a son for (Allah) Most Gracious. For it is not consonant with the majesty of (Allah) Most Gracious that He should beget a son. Not one of the beings in the heavens and the earth but must come to (Allah) Most Gracious as a slave. He does take an account of them (all), and has numbered them (all) exactly. And every one of them will come to Him singly on the Day of Judgment."
(Maryam 19:88-95)

"He ['Isa] was no more than a slave: We granted Our favour to him, and we made him an example to the Children of Israel." (al-Zukhruf 43:59)

"To Him belongs whosoever is in the heavens and on earth. And those who are near to Him (i.e. the angels) are not too proud to worship Him, nor are they weary (of His worship). They glorify His Praises night and day, (and) they never slacken (to do so)." (al-Anbiya' 21:19-20)

"The Messiah will never be proud to reject to be a slave to Allah, nor the angels who are near (to Allah). And whosoever rejects His worship and is proud, then He will gather them all together unto Himself. So, as for those who believed and did deeds of righteousness, He will give their (due) rewards and more out of His bounty. But as for those who refuse His worship and were proud, He will punish them with a painful torment. And they will not find for themselves besides Allah any protector or helper." (al-Nisa' 4:172-173)

"And your Lord says: 'Call on Me: I will answer your (Prayer): but those who are too arrogant to worship Me will surely find themselves in Hell - in humiliation!'" (Ghafir 40:60)

"Among His Signs are the Night and the Day, and the sun and the moon. Adore not the sun and the moon, but adore Allah Who created them, if it is Him you wish to worship. But if the (Unbelievers) are arrogant, (no matter): for in the presence of your Lord are those who celebrate His praises by night and by day, and they never flag (nor feel themselves above it)." (Fussilat 41:37-38)

"And bring your Lord to remembrance in your (very) soul, with humility and in reverence, without loudness in words, in the mornings and evenings; and be not of those who are heedless. Those who are near to your Lord, disdain not to do Him worship: they celebrate His praises, and bow down before Him." (al-A'raf 7:205-206)

Many Messengers, one Message

There are many *ayat* in the Qur'an which describe the best of creation as being those who are slaves of Allah, and condemn those who rebel against this "enslavement". Allah tells us that He sent all of His Messengers with this same message:

"Not a messenger did We send before you without this inspiration sent by Us to him: that there is no god but I; therefore worship and serve only Me." (al-Anbiya' 21:25)

"For We assuredly sent amongst every People a messenger, (with the Command), 'Worship Allah and eschew [shun] evil'..." (al-Nahl 16:36)

"O My slaves Who believe! Truly, spacious is My earth: therefore serve Me (and Me alone)!" (al-'Ankabut 29:56)

"...and fear Me, and Me alone." (al-Baqarah 2:41)

"O people! Worship your Guardian-Lord, Who created you and those who came before you, that you may become righteous." (al-Baqarah 2:21)

"I have only created jinns and men, that they may worship Me." (al-Dhariyat 51:56)

"Say (O Muhammad): 'Verily, I am commanded to worship Allah (Alone) by obeying Him and doing religious deeds sincerely for Allah's sake only and not to show off, and not to set up rivals with Him in worship. And I am commanded (this) in order that I may be the first of those who submit themselves to Allah (in Islam) as Muslims.' Say (O Muhammad): 'Verily, if I disobey my Lord, I am afraid of the torment of a great Day.' Say (O Muhammad): 'Allah Alone I worship by doing religious deeds sincerely for His sake only and not to show off, and not to set up rivals with Him in worship.' So worship what you like besides Him..." (al-Zumar 39:11-15)

Each of the Messengers began his message with the call to worship Allah, as Nuh 🕮 and messengers after him (upon all of whom be peace) said:

"*'Worship Allah! You have no other god but Him. Will you not fear (Him)?'*" (al-Mu'minun 23:32)

It was reported in *al-Musnad* from Ibn 'Umar that the Prophet 🕮 said:

"I have been sent with a sword just before the Hour, so that Allah will be worshipped alone, with no partners attributed to Him. My provision has been placed in the shadow of my spear, and humiliation has been allotted for the one who goes against my command." *(Al-Bukhari and Abu Dawud)*

Sincere slaves saved from Shaytan

Allah explained that the sincere worshippers and slaves of Allah are the ones who will be saved from the *sayi'at* (evil deeds) which Shaytan makes look attractive:

"Iblis [Shaytan] said: 'O my Lord! Because you have put me in the wrong, I will make (wrong) fair-seeming to them on the earth, and I will put them all in the wrong - Except for Your servants among them, sincere and purified (by Your Grace).'" (al-Hijr 15:39-40)

"(Allah) said: 'This (Way of My sincere slaves) is indeed a Way that leads straight to Me. For over My servants no authority shall you have except such as put themselves in the wrong and follow you.'" (al-Hijr 15:41-42)

"(Iblis) said: 'Then, by Your power, I will put them all in the wrong - Except Your slaves amongst them, sincere and purified (by Your Grace).'" (Sad 38:82-83)

Concerning Yusuf ﷺ, Allah says:

> *"...Thus (did We order) that We might turn away from him (all) evil and shameful deeds: for he was one of Our slaves, sincere and purified."* (Yusuf 12:24)

Allah says:

> *"Glory to Allah! (He is free) from the things they ascribe (to Him)! Not (so do) the slaves of Allah, sincere and devoted."* (al–Saffat 37:159–160)

> *"No authority has he (Shaytan) over those who believe and put their trust in their Lord. His authority is over those only who take him as patron and who join partners with Allah."* (al–Nahl 16:99–100)

Chosen ones are His slaves

Allah has described everyone whom He has chosen of His creation as being *'abd* (His true slave):

> *"And remember Our slaves, Ibrahim, Ishaq and Ya'qub, (all) owners of strength (in worshipping Us) and (also) of religious understanding. Verily, We did choose them by granting them (a good thing - i.e.) the remembrance of the home (in the Hereafter). And they are with Us, verily, of the chosen and the best!"* (Sad 38:45-47)

> *"...and remember Our slave Dawud, endued with power. Verily, he was ever oft-returning in all matters and in repentance (toward Allah)."* (Sad 38:17)

> (Of Sulayman): *"...How excellent (a) slave! Verily, he was ever oft-returning in repentance to Us!"* (Sad 38:30)

> (Of Ayyub): *"...How excellent (a) slave!..."* (Sad 38:44)

"And remember Our slave Ayyub, when he invoked his Lord..."
(Sad 38:41)

"O offspring of those whom We carried (in the ship) with Nuh! Verily, He was a grateful slave." (al–Isra' 17:3)

"Glorified (and Exalted) be He Who took His slave (Muhammad) for a journey by night from al-Masjid al-Haram (at Makkah) to the farthest mosque (at Jerusalem)..." (al–Isra' 17:1)

This (Jerusalem) was the first *Qiblah* (direction of prayer), which Allah made special by making worship there five hundred times better in reward. Some people think that *al-Masjid al-Aqsa* is just the Rock and the Dome over it, but this is not the case.

And Allah said:

"When the slave of Allah (Muhammad) stood up invoking (his Lord) in prayer to Him..." (al-Jinn 72:19)

"And if you are in doubt concerning that which We have sent down to Our slave (Muhammad)..." (al–Baqarah 2:23)

"So did Allah convey the Inspiration to His slave (Muhammad)" (al–Najm 53:10)

"A spring wherefrom the slaves of Allah will drink..." (al-Insan 76:6)

"And the slaves of the Most Beneficent are those who walk on the earth in humility and sedateness..." (al-Furqan 25:63)

There are many further examples like this in the Qur'an.

"And the slaves of the Most Beneficent are those who walk on the earth in humility and sedateness..."

(al–Furqan 25:63)

Al-ʿUbudiyyah

Part Three

"And among them are men who slander you [the Prophet] in the matter of (the distribution of) alms. If they are given part thereof, they are pleased, but if not, behold! They are indignant!"

(al-Tawbah 9:58)

Different levels of *iman*

If the above is clear, then it is obvious that people will differ greatly in this regard, i.e. in the reality of *iman*. Thus they may be divided into two types: rank-and-file *('am)* and elite *(khass),* and the relationship of Allah to different people will differ accordingly.

Slaves of the material world

Hence in this *ummah* the issue of *shirk* is subtler than the noise made by the footsteps of an ant. According to a *sahih hadith,* the Prophet 鷺 said: "Wretched is the slave of the *dirham,* and the slave of the *dinar,* and the slave of velvet and brocade. He is doomed to failure. If he is afflicted with a thorn, may he not be able to remove it. If he is given, he is content, but if he is not given, he becomes angry."

The Prophet 鷺 described such a person as being a slave of the *dirham* and *dinar,* and of velvet and brocade, and stated that he is doomed to failure; he also prayed that if such a person were pricked by a thorn (a minor affliction), he would not be able to remove it.

This is the situation of a person who may be afflicted by calamity, but is not able to overcome it, because he is doomed to failure. So he can neither achieve his aim nor rid himself of the thing he hates. This is the situation of one who is a slave to wealth and material possessions, who was described as being content when he is given something and angry when it is withheld from him. Allah says:

"And among them are men who slander you [the Prophet] in the matter of (the distribution of) alms. If they are given part thereof, they are pleased, but if not, behold! They are indignant!" (al-Tawbah 9:58)

Neither their pleasure nor their anger is for the sake of Allah.

Slaves to their desires

This is also the situation of a man who is attached to a position of leadership or to a beautiful image, or any other kind of desire. If he gets what he wants, he is happy, but if he does not achieve it, he becomes angry. So he is a slave to whatever it is that he desires, because enslavement is essentially the enslavement of the heart: whatever the heart is enthralled by, is the thing of which the heart is a slave.

For this reason, the Arab poets said:
"The slave is free so long as he is content, and the free man is a slave so long as he is greedy."
"I followed my desires and they enslaved me. If only I had been content with my lot, I would be free."

It is said that greed and longing are like chains around the neck and shackles on the feet. Even if the chain is removed from the neck, the feet are still shackled.

It was reported that 'Umar ibn al-Khattab ﷺ said, "Greed is poverty, and resignation is wealth. When any one of you gives up hope of something, he becomes independent of it."

This is something which anyone can feel in his heart, for when he gives up hope of something, he no longer wants it or longs for it; he no longer feels in need of it or of the one who can help him to get it. If he longs for and hopes for something, then his heart is attached to it, and he feels that he is in need of it and of the one who he thinks can be the means to this end. This is the case in matters of wealth and power and beautiful images or people, etc.

Seeking sustenance from Allah, not other people

Ibrahim ﷺ advised, *"...Then seek sustenance with Allah, worship Him, and be grateful to Him: to Him will be your return."* (al-'Ankabut 29:17)

Everyone needs provision and sustenance *(rizq)*. If a person seeks this *rizq* from Allah, then he will be a slave to Allah and feel in need of Him. If he seeks it from some created being, he will be enslaved by and feel in need of that being. This is why it is basically forbidden to ask for anything from another created being, although it is permitted to do so in cases of necessity. There are many *ahadith* forbidding this kind of asking from people, for example:

"One of you will keep on asking until he comes on the Day of Resurrection with no flesh on his face." *(Al-Bukhari, Muslim and al-Nisa'i)*

"Whoever begs from people when he has enough to make him independent, his begging will appear on the Day of Resurrection as scratches or gashes on his face." *(Al-Tabarani)*

"Begging is not permitted except for the one who is burdened with heavy debts, or who owes blood-money, or who is suffering from crushing poverty." *(Abu Dawud and al-Bayhaqi)*

"If any one of you were to take a rope and go and gather wood, that would be better for him than asking people (for help), which they may or may not give." *(al-Bukhari and Ibn Majah)*

"Whatever wealth you receive without asking for it or hoping for it, take it, and whatever you do not receive, do not wish for it." *(Al-Bukhari, Muslim and al-Nisa'i)*

The Prophet ﷺ did not like anyone to ask for anything, whether he asked for it verbally or by longing in his heart. According to a *sahih hadith* he said:

"Whoever wants to be independent, Allah will make him independent. Whoever wants not to have to ask people for anything, Allah will help him to be free of that. Whoever wants to be patient, Allah will give him patience. Nobody has ever been given anything better and more abundant than patience." *(Al-Bukhari, Muslim, Malik, Abu Dawud, al-Nisa'i and al-Tirmidhi)*

The Prophet ﷺ advised his closest Companions not to ask anyone for anything. It was reported in *al-Musnad* that if Abu Bakr ﷺ dropped his whip (whilst riding), he would not ask anyone to hand it to him, but he would say, "My close friend (i.e. the Prophet ﷺ) commanded me not to ask people for anything." Muslim and others reported from 'Awf ibn Malik that the Prophet ﷺ received *bay'ah* (oath of allegiance) from him with a group of people, and whispered to them that they should not ask people for anything. Some of the people of that group, if they happened to drop a whip (whilst riding) would not even ask anyone to hand it to them.

Many *ayat* and *ahadith* indicate that we should ask from the Creator, not from other created beings. For example, Allah says:

> "So when you have finished (from your occupation), then stand up for Allah's worship (i.e. stand up for prayer), and to your Lord (Alone) turn (all your intentions and hopes and) your invocations." (al-Sharh 94:7–8)

And the Prophet ﷺ said to Ibn 'Abbas, "If you must ask for anything, ask Allah, and if you seek help, seek help from Allah." *(Al-Tirmidhi, Ahmad and al-Hakim)*

Ibrahim عليه السلام said, *"...Then seek sustenance from Allah..."* (al-'Ankabut 29:17). In Arabic, this phrase reads *fabta'ghu 'ind Allah il-rizq*, which translates literally as "then seek with Allah sustenance". The prepositional phrase *'ind Allah* ("with Allah") comes first for a reason, which is to indicate exclusivity, as if to say: do not seek sustenance except from Allah. Allah also says, *"...and ask Allah of His Bounty"* (al-Nisa' 4:32).

Complaining only to Allah

Man needs to obtain his provision and other needs, and to protect himself from harm. In both cases, he should call on Allah. He should not ask for provision from anyone other than Allah, and he should not complain to anyone other than Allah. As Ya'qub ﷺ said, *"I only complain of my distraction and anguish to Allah..."* (Yusuf 12:86).

In the Qur'an, Allah has mentioned goodly forsaking, goodly forgiveness and goodly patience. It was said that goodly forsaking is to forsake or boycott without doing harm; goodly forgiveness is to forgive without rebuking; and goodly patience is to be patient without complaining to any other person or created being. When Ahmad ibn Hanbal was sick, he was told that Tawus used to hate the sound of a sick person's groaning, and would say, "This is a complaint", so Ahmad never groaned until the day he died.

Complaining to the Creator, on the other hand, does not contradict the idea of goodly patience. For Ya'qub ﷺ said, *"Patience is most fitting (for me)"* (Yusuf 12:83), but he also said, *"I only complain of my distraction and anguish to Allah..."* (Yusuf 12:86).

'Umar ibn al-Khattab ﷺ used to recite *Surahs Yunus, Yusuf* and *al-Nahl* during Fajr prayer. When he reached this *ayah,* he wept so much that his sobs could be heard in the last rows of the congregation.

Musa ﷺ used to pray, "O Allah, to You be all praise and to You (Alone) do I complain. You are the (only) One Whom I ask for help, in You I seek refuge and upon You I rely. There is no strength or power except in You."

One of the *du'a's* which the Prophet ﷺ said when the people of al-Ta'if did what they did to him was, "O Allah, to You I complain of my weakness and helplessness, and of the people's caring nothing for me. O Most Merciful of those who show mercy, You are the Lord of the dispossessed and You are my Lord. O Allah, to whom will you leave me? To a stranger who will push me away and mistreat me, or to an enemy to whom You have given power over me? As long as You are not angry with me, nothing else matters, but still Your protection and help are better for me. I seek refuge in the light of Your countenance, which lights up the darkness and sets right the affairs of this world and the Hereafter, from Your anger and wrath descending upon me. I seek Your forgiveness until You are pleased with me. There is no strength and no power except in Allah." According to another report, he said, "There is no strength and no power except in You."

Hope in the mercy and bounty of Allah

The more hope a slave has in the merciful bounty of Allah and His ability to supply his needs and protect him from harm, the stronger his feeling of servitude *('ubudiyyah)* to Him grows, and the more free he becomes from everything other than Allah. If he pins his hopes on any created being, he is bound to be enslaved by it, but when he places no hope in it, his heart is independent of it. As it was said: Be independent of whomever you wish, and you will be his equal; do a favour to whomever you wish, and you will be his superior; be in need of whomever you wish and you will be his prisoner. So when the slave rests his hopes on Allah, he is bound to be a true slave to Him, but if his heart refuses to ask from Allah and put its hope in Him, it will also turn away from true worship and servitude, especially if he puts his trust in some created being rather than in the Creator. His heart then will be dependent upon his position of leadership and his troops, followers and servants, or on his family and friends, or on his wealth and savings, or on his leaders and superiors, such as a master, king, *shaykh,* employer or other mere mortal. Allah says:

"And put your trust in Him Who lives and dies not; and celebrate His praise; and enough is He to be acquainted with the faults of His servants." (al-Furqan 25:58)

Servitude to other than Allah

Everyone who depends on other people to help him, provide for him or guide him is subjugated to them in his heart, and is therefore in a state of servitude towards them, even if it appears on the surface that he is in charge of them and directing their affairs. The wise man looks at realities, not at outward appearances. If a man's heart is dependent on a woman – even if she is permissible for him – he will remain her prisoner and she can direct him as she wishes, even though on the outside it may appear that he is in charge of her because he is her husband or master. He will be her prisoner and slave, especially if she knows how dependent he is on her, how much he loves her and how irreplaceable she is in his eyes. Then she will be able to rule him in the manner of a despot who cannot be got rid of. It is even worse than that, for the enslavement of the heart is more serious than the enslavement of the body, for the one whose body is enslaved and imprisoned will not care so long as his heart is free and at peace, and he may even be able to find a way out.

Following the heart

But if the heart, which is the controller of the body, is enslaved and attached to something other than Allah, this is true humiliation and total imprisonment, for servitude is that to which the heart is attached.

The enslavement and imprisonment of the heart form the basis of reward and punishment. If a Muslim is imprisoned by a *kafir* or enslaved by an evildoer unjustly, this will not harm him so long as he carries out his duties towards Allah as much as he can. If he is forced to speak the words of *kufr,* and does so whilst his heart remains firm in its faith, this will not harm him either. But the person whose heart is enslaved becomes a slave to something other than Allah, and this will harm him, even if outwardly he appears to be in control of others.

True freedom

True freedom is the freedom of the heart and true servitude is the servitude of the heart, just as true richness is contentment with one's lot. The Prophet ﷺ said:

> "Richness is not having a lot of wealth; richness is being content with one's lot." *(Al-Bukhari and Muslim)*

This is the case if his heart is enslaved by a woman who is permissible for him, but if his heart is enslaved by someone who is forbidden for him, whether a woman or a boy, this is an incomparable punishment.

These lovers of images are the people who will be most severely punished and least rewarded. If a person's heart remains attached to and enslaved by the image he loves, he will combine all kinds of evil and corruption, to an extent known only to Allah. Even if he does not commit the major sin [of illicit sexual contact], his heart will still be attached to her, and this is worse for him than committing a (lesser) sin and then repenting from it, whereupon all trace of it is lifted from his heart.

One of the main causes for this miserable situation is turning away from Allah, for once the heart has tasted worship of Allah and sincerity towards Him, nothing will be sweeter to it than that, nothing will be more delightful or more precious. No one leaves his beloved except for another one whom he loves even more, or for fear of something else. The heart will give up corrupt love in favour of true love, or for fear of harm.

Allah protects those who love Him

Allah says, describing Yusuf ﷺ:

> *"...thus (did We order) that We might turn away from him (all) evil and shameful deeds: for He was one of Our slaves, sincere and purified."* (Yusuf 12:24)

Allah directs away from His slave all that He dislikes in the way of inclinations towards images and attachment to them, and He protects him from evil and shameful deeds by his sincerity towards Allah. This is why before he tastes the sweetness of true servitude and sincerity towards Allah, he will be overwhelmed by his desires, but once he tastes the sweetness of sincerity and it becomes well established in his heart, he will be able to control his desires without any further need for treatment. Allah says:

> *"...Prayer restrains from shameful and unjust deeds; and remembrance of Allah is the greatest (thing in life) without doubt..."* (al-'Ankabut 29:45)

Prayer offers protection from something bad, namely shameful and unjust deeds, and helps one to achieve something good, namely remembrance of Allah. Achieving this good thing is more important than protecting oneself from that bad thing, for remembering Allah and worshipping Him with all one's heart is the ultimate aim, whereas protecting oneself from evil is just the means to an end. The heart is created in such a way that it loves and seeks truth, so when an evil thought comes along, it pushes it away lest it ruin the heart just as a field of crops may be ruined by weeds.

Purifying the soul

Hence Allah says:

> *"Truly he succeeds that purifies it [the soul], and he fails that corrupts it!"* (al-Shams 91:9-10)

"But those will prosper who purify themselves, and glorify the name of their Guardian-Lord, and (lift their hearts) in Prayer." (al-A'la 87:14–15)

"Say to the believing men that they should lower their gaze and guard their modesty: that will make for greater purity for them..." (al-Nur 24:30)

"...And were it not for the grace and mercy of Allah on you, not one of you would ever have been pure..." (al-Nur 24:21)

Allah has made lowering one's gaze and guarding one's modesty the strongest means of purifying one's soul. He has explained that refraining from shameful deeds purifies one's soul, and purifying one's soul includes ridding oneself of all kinds of evil, including shameful deeds, injustice, *shirk,* lying and so on.

Enslaved by worldly ambitions

The one who seeks power and leadership is enslaved to those who can help him to achieve this, even if it outwardly appears that he is in charge of them and is the one who issues commands to them. In reality, his hopes and fears rest on them, so he gives them money and positions of authority and overlooks their mistakes so that they will obey him and help him. Although he appears to be the boss giving orders, in fact he is a slave to them.

Indeed, the truth is that each of them is a slave to the other, for both have forsaken true enslavement to Allah. If their co-operation to gain power on earth is unjust, then they are just like those who co-operate in shameful deeds or banditry. Each one of them, because of the desires by which he is enslaved, is a slave to the other.

This also applies to the one who seeks wealth, for that wealth has enslaved him. Wealth is of two types. The first is that which a person needs for his food, drink, housing, wife and so on, which he should seek from Allah so that he can use it for his own needs, just as he may seek a donkey to ride, a carpet to sit on, even the facilities with which to answer the call of nature, without being enslaved by it, or becoming *"very impatient, fretful when evil touches him and niggardly when good reaches him"* (al-Ma'arij 70:19-21). The other type of wealth is that which a person does not need, and so his heart should not become attached to it, for if that happens, he will be enslaved by it. Then he may become dependent on something other than Allah, and he will no longer be truly enslaved to Allah or relying upon Him. Now there will be an element of being enslaved by and relying upon something other than Allah. This is the person who is most aptly described by the *hadith*:

> "Wretched is the slave of the dirham, and the slave of the dinar, and the slave of velvet and brocade." *(Al-Bukhari and Ibn Majah)*

This refers to the one who is a slave to those things. If he asks Allah for something, and He gives it, he is happy, but if Allah withholds it, he becomes angry. But the true slave of Allah is happy with that which pleases Allah, and is angry with and hates that which displeases Allah. He loves that which Allah and His Messenger love, and hates that which Allah and His Messenger hate. He befriends and supports the friends of Allah, and shows enmity towards the enemies of Allah. This is the one whose faith is perfected, as in the *hadith*:

> "Whoever loves for the sake of Allah, hates for the sake of Allah, gives for the sake of Allah and withholds for the sake of Allah, has perfected his faith." *(Abu Dawud)*

Bonds of faith

The Prophet ﷺ also said:
> "The strongest bond of faith is love for the sake of Allah and hate for the sake of Allah." *(Ahmad and al-Tabarani)*

In *al-Sahih* it is reported that the Prophet ﷺ said:
> "There are three things, whoever attains them will find the sweetness of faith: the one to whom Allah and His Messenger are more beloved than anything else; the one who loves another only for the sake of Allah; and the one who would hate to go back to *kufr* after Allah has saved him from it as he would hate to be thrown into fire." *(Agreed upon)*

The person who has achieved this goes along with what his Lord loves and hates, so Allah and His Messenger are dearer to him than all else and he loves other created beings only for the sake of Allah, and not for any other reason. This is the one who has perfected his love for Allah, for loving that which one's beloved loves is the perfection of love for one's beloved. So he loves the Prophets of Allah and the friends of Allah because they are carrying out their duties towards Allah, not for any other reason. He loves them for the sake of Allah, and not for any other reason. Allah says:
> *"...soon will Allah produce a people whom He will love as they love Him - lowly with the Believers, mighty against the Rejecters (disbelievers)..."* (al-Ma'idah 5:54)

Hence Allah says:
> *"Say: 'If you do love Allah, follow me: Allah will love you...'"* (Al 'Imran 3:31)

The Messenger only commands that which Allah loves, and he only forbids that which Allah hates. He only does that which Allah loves and tells about that which Allah loves people to believe in.

If you love Allah, you must follow His Messenger

Whoever loves Allah must follow the Messenger, believe in what he says, obey what he commands, and emulate what he does. Whoever does this does what Allah loves, and so Allah will love him.

Allah has made two signs of those who love him: following His Messenger, and striving in *jihad* for His sake. The true essence of *jihad* is striving to achieve that which Allah loves of faith and righteous deeds, and to repel what Allah hates of *kufr*, immorality and sin. Allah says:

> "Say: 'If it be that your fathers, your sons, your brothers, your mates, or your kindred; the wealth that you have gained; the commerce in which you fear a decline; or the dwellings in which you delight - are dearer to you than Allah, or His Messenger, or the striving in His Cause - then wait until Allah brings about His Decision...'" (al–Tawbah 9:24)

Allah has issued this threat as a warning to those whose families and wealth are more beloved to them than Allah and His Messenger, and *jihad* for His sake. Indeed, it is proven that the Prophet 🌺 said:

> "By the One in Whose hand is my soul, none of you truly believes until I am more beloved to him than his child, his father and all the people." *(Al-Bukhari and Muslim)*

It is reported in *al-Sahih* that 'Umar ibn al-Khattab 🌺 said, "O Messenger of Allah, by Allah you are dearer to me than everything except my own self." He said, "No, O 'Umar, (you are not right) until I am dearer to you than your own self." He said, "By Allah, you are dearer to me than my own self." He said, "Now (you are right), O 'Umar." *(Al-Bukhari and Muslim)*

True love can only be perfected by loyalty to the beloved, by loving what he loves and hating what he hates. Allah loves *iman* (faith) and *taqwa* (piety), and He hates *kufr*, immorality and sin.

It is known that love influences the will in the heart. The stronger that love becomes, the more the heart will seek that which Allah loves. If the love is perfected, there must needs be the firm resolve to do good deeds which are loved, if the person is able to do them. If he is not able to do them, he will do as much of them as he can, and he will receive a reward equivalent to that of the one who does them, as the Prophet ﷺ said:

> "Whoever calls to right guidance will have a reward like that of the one who follows it, without it detracting from (the latter's) reward in the slightest. And whoever calls to misguidance will bear a burden of sin equivalent to that of those who follow it, without it detracting from (the latter's) punishment in the slightest." *(Muslim)*

And he said (whilst on a military campaign), "In Madinah there are men, who did not walk in a place or cross a valley, but they were with you." They asked, "They are in Madinah?" He said, "They are in Madinah, but they have an excuse (a valid reason why they did not come out to fight)." *(Agreed upon)*

Jihad

Jihad means to do one's utmost, to do all that one possibly can, to do that which Allah loves and to repel that which He hates. If a slave fails to do anything he is capable of in *jihad,* this is indicative of some weakness or imperfection in his love for Allah and His Messenger.

It is known that usually one cannot achieve what one loves except by putting up with hardship, whether the object of one's love is worthy or otherwise. Those who love wealth, power and images do not attain them except by suffering some damage or harm in worldly terms, as well as the harm that will befall them in this world and the next. If a person who claims to love Allah and His Messenger is unable to put up with hardship, which even wise people who do not love Allah realise they

74

must put up with in order to achieve their goals, this indicates some weakness or imperfection in his love for Allah.

It is known that the true believer is overflowing with love for Allah, as Allah says:

"Yet there are men who take (for worship) others besides Allah as equals (with Allah): they love them as they should love Allah, but those of Faith are overflowing in their love for Allah…" (al-Baqarah 2:165)

Indeed, a person who loves Allah - if he is weak in understanding and fails to grasp the correct concepts - may follow a path that does not achieve the desired goal. Such paths are worthless even if the person's love for Allah is sincere and praiseworthy. So how must it be if his love is corrupt and faulty (focused on the wrong thing), and the path is one that leads nowhere, as in the case of those reckless souls who pursue wealth, power and images, loving things that harm them and do not achieve their goals? What should be sought is the path followed by the people of sound understanding in order to reach the desired goal.

True *'ubudiyyah* to Allah

Once this is understood clearly, we will see that the more the heart increases in love, the more it increases in servitude, and vice versa, and so it gives Allah priority over all else. The heart is inherently dependent on Allah in two ways: from the point of view of worship, which is the ultimate goal, and from the point of view of seeking His help and relying upon Him, which are the means to that end. The heart cannot be sound, or succeed, or find joy, or be happy, or feel pleasure, or be good, or be at peace, or find tranquillity, except by worshipping its Lord, loving Him and returning to Him. Even if it attains all that it can enjoy of created things, it will not feel at peace or find tranquillity, because it has an inherent need for its Lord, for He is the focus of its worship, love and seeking, and this is the only way to attain joy, happiness, pleasure, peace and tranquillity.

Necessity of seeking the help of Allah

This can only be attained with the help of Allah, for no one is able to help a person achieve this except Allah. So man needs to realise the true meaning of the words, *"You do we worship, and Your help we seek"* (al-Fatihah 1:5). For if a person is helped to attain what he loves, seeks, desires and wants, but he does not worship Allah, he will never achieve anything but sorrow, regret and suffering. He can never be free of the pain and hardship of this life except through loving Allah sincerely, so that Allah becomes his ultimate desire and he loves Him for what He is, and he loves anyone or anything else only for His sake, and he does not love anything for its own sake except Allah. If he does not achieve this (level of love), he has not properly understood the true meaning of *"la ilaha ill-Allah"* or of *Tawhid* or of *'ubudiyyah* or of loving Allah. There is something lacking in his *iman* and *Tawhid,* and he will suffer pain, regret and anguish accordingly.

If he strives for this purpose without seeking the help of Allah or putting his trust in Him and depending on Him to help him achieve it, he will never achieve it. For what Allah wills happens, and what He does not will does not happen. Man is in need of Allah, for He is the One Who is sought and loved, needed and worshipped, and He is the One Who is to be asked for help and relied upon. He is his *ilah,* besides Whom he has no other god, and He is his *Rabb,* besides Whom he has no other lord.

True servitude to Allah *('ubudiyyah)* cannot be achieved and perfected except when these two concepts (of *ilah* and *rabb)* are properly understood. When a person loves something other than Allah for its own sake, or turns to something other than Allah to ask for help, he is a slave to what he loves, and a slave to whatever he puts his hope in. If he does not love anyone for his own sake except Allah, and does not love anything but Allah except for His sake, and he never puts his hope in anything other than Allah, and when he resorts to any means he realises that Allah is the One Who has created it, decreed it and subjugated it to him, and that Allah is the Controller, Creator and Subjugator of all that is in heaven and on earth, and that he is in need of Him – then he has attained true servitude to Allah in accordance with his allotted share.

In this regard, people are of differing levels, according to the level of their hope and fear, and to an extent known only to Allah.

The best people

The best and most perfect of people, the highest and closest to Allah, the strongest and most rightly-guided, are those whose servitude to Allah is most perfect in this regard.

This is the true essence of the religion of Islam, with which Allah sent His Messengers and revealed His Books. It means to submit oneself to Allah and to no other, for the one who submits himself to Allah and to someone or something else is a *mushrik,* and the one who refuses to submit to Him is arrogant and stubbornly proud. It is reported in *al-Sahih* that the Prophet ﷺ said that no one will enter Paradise who has an atom's weight of pride in his heart (Muslim) just as no one will remain in Hell forever who has an atom's weight of faith in his heart. So stubborn pride is regarded as the opposite of faith, and pride contradicts true *'ubudiyyah.* It is reported in *al-Sahih* that the Prophet ﷺ said, "Allah says: 'Might is My garment and pride is My cloak. Whoever competes with me in either of them, I will punish him'" *(Muslim and Abu Dawud).* Might and pride are characteristics of divinity, and pride is higher than might, which is why it is likened to a cloak or upper garment *(rida')*, whilst might is likened to the lower garment *(izar)*.

For this reason, the slogan or motif of the prayer, *adhan* and the two 'Eids is the *Takbir (Allahu akbar)*. It is *mustahabb* (recommended) to recite *Takbir* in high places, such as al-Safa' and al-Marwa, and elsewhere, when mounting one's riding-beast, and so on, and when putting out fires, even if they have grown big. When the *adhan* is recited, the Shaytan flees. Allah says:

> *"And your Lord says: 'Call on Me: I will answer your (Prayer): but those who are too arrogant to serve Me will surely find themselves in Hell - in humiliation!'"* (Ghafir 40:60)

Every person must have a focus for his love

Everyone who is too proud and arrogant to worship Allah inevitably worships something else, for man is sensitive and is always motivated by ideas. It is reported in *al-Sahih* that the Prophet 🕮 said, "The truest of names are Harith and Hammam." Harith means "one who is active and always doing things", and Hammam means "one who is always looking for things to do". Ideas are the beginning of will, and man always has a will which inevitably needs an objective and a focus. Every person must have an ultimate aim which is the focus of his love and will. If a person does not have Allah as the focus of his love and will, and is too proud and arrogant, he will inevitably have something else as his focus, which will enslave him instead of Allah, and he will be its slave, whether it is wealth, power or images, or something that he takes as a god instead of Allah, such as the sun, moon, stars, idols, graves of Prophets and righteous people, or angels and Prophets whom he takes as lords, or anything else that is worshipped instead of Allah.

If he is a slave to anything other than Allah, he is a *mushrik,* and everyone who is stubbornly proud and arrogant is a *mushrik.* Hence Pharaoh was one of the most arrogant of all people and most stubborn in his refusal to worship Allah, and he was a *mushrik.* Allah says:

"Of old, We sent Musa, with Our Signs and an Authority Manifest, to Pharaoh, Haman and Qarun; but they called (him) 'a sorcerer telling lies!'... Musa said: 'I have indeed called upon my Lord and your Lord (for protection) from every arrogant one who believes not in the Day of Account!'...Thus does Allah seal up every heart - of arrogant and obstinate transgressors." (Ghafir 40:23-24, 27, 35)

"(Remember also) Qarun, Pharaoh and Haman: there came to them Musa with Clear Signs, but they behaved with insolence on the earth; yet they could not overreach (Us)." (al-'Ankabut 29:39)

"Truly Pharaoh elated himself in the land and broke up its people into sections, depressing a small group among them: their sons he slew, but he kept alive their females..." (al-Qasas 28:4)

"And they [Pharaoh and his people] rejected those Signs in iniquity and arrogance, though their souls were convinced thereof: so see what was the end of those who acted corruptly!" (al-Naml 27:14)

There are many other similar references in the Qur'an. Allah described Pharaoh as a *mushrik* in the *ayah:*

"Said the chiefs of Pharaoh's people: 'Will you leave Musa and his people, to spread mischief in the land, and to abandon you and your gods?'..." (al-A'raf 7:127)

Indeed, all the evidence indicates that the more arrogant a man is in his refusal to worship Allah, the more guilty he is of associating others with Allah, because the more arrogant he is in his refusal to worship Allah, the more dependent he becomes on the desired goal which is the ultimate focus of his heart and so he begins to worship that which has enslaved him.

The heart can never be independent of other created beings unless Allah is its master and it worships none other than Him, seeks help from none other than Him, places its trust in none other than Him, rejoices only in that which He loves, despises only that which He hates, loves only for the sake of Allah, hates nothing except for the sake of Allah, does not give except for the sake of Allah and does not withhold except for the sake of Allah. The more sincere a person is towards Allah, the more perfect his *'ubudiyyah* becomes and the more independent he becomes from other created beings. The more perfect his servitude towards Allah becomes, the more free he becomes of arrogance and *shirk*.

Shirk and arrogance

Shirk is more common among the Christians, and arrogance is more common among the Jews. Concerning the Christians, Allah says:

> *"They take their priests and their anchorites to be their lords in derogation of Allah, and (they take as their Lord) Christ, the son of Mary; yet they were commanded to worship but One God: there is no god but He. Praise and glory be to Him: (far is He) from having the partners they associate (with Him)."* (al-Tawbah 9:31)

Concerning the Jews, Allah says:

> *"...Is it that whenever there comes to you a Messenger with what you yourselves desire not, you are puffed up with pride? - some you called impostors, and others you slay!"* (al-Baqarah 2:87)

And Allah says:

> *"Those who behave arrogantly on the earth in defiance of right - them will I turn away from My Signs: even if they see all the Signs, they will not believe*

in them; and if they see the way of right conduct, they will not adopt it as the Way; but if they see the way of error, that is the Way they will adopt..." (al-A'raf 7:146)

Because arrogant pride is the same as *shirk*, and *shirk* is opposed to Islam and is the sin that Allah will not forgive, Allah says:

"Allah forgives not that partners should be set up with Him: but He forgives anything else, to whom He pleases: to set up partners with Allah is to devise a sin most heinous indeed." (al-Nisa' 4:48)

"Allah forgives not (the sin of) joining other gods with Him; but He forgives whom He pleases other sins than this: one who joins other gods with Allah, has strayed far, far away (from the Right)." (al-Nisa' 4:116)

Because of this, all the Prophets were sent with the religion of Islam, which is the only religion that Allah will accept. He will not accept any other religion, not from the earlier generations nor the latter generations.

Nuh ﷺ said: *"But if you turn back, (consider): No reward have I asked of you: my reward is only due from Allah, and I have been commanded to be of those who submit to Allah's will (in Islam)."* (Yunus 10:72)

Allah said:

"And who turns away from the religion of Ibrahim but such as debase their souls with folly? Him We chose and rendered pure in this world: and he will be in the Hereafter in the ranks of the Righteous. Behold! His Lord said to him: 'Bow (your will to Me)': He said: 'I bow (my will) to the Lord and Cherisher of the Universe.' And this was the legacy that Ibrahim left to his sons, and so did Ya'qub: 'O my sons! Allah has chosen the Faith for you; then die not except in the state of submission (to Allah).'" (al-Baqarah 2:130-132)

Yusuf ﷺ said: *"'...Take my soul (at death) as one submitting to Your Will (as a Muslim), and unite me with the righteous.'"* (Yusuf 12:101)

Musa عَلَيْهِ said: *"'O my people! If you do (really) believe in Allah, then in Him put your trust if you submit (your will to His).' They said: 'In Allah we put our trust...'"* (Yunus 10:83–84)

Allah said:

"It was We Who revealed the Law (to Musa): therein was guidance and light. By its standards have been judged the Jews, by the Prophets who bowed (as in Islam) to Allah's Will..." (al-Ma'idah 5:44)

Bilqis said: *"'O my Lord! I have indeed wronged my soul: I do (now) submit (in Islam), with Solomon, to the Lord of the Worlds.'"* (al-Naml 27:44)

Allah said:

"And behold! I inspired the Disciples to have faith in Me and My Messenger; they said, 'We have faith, and bear witness that we bow to Allah as Muslims.'" (al-Ma'idah 5:111)

"The religion before Allah is Islam (submission to His Will)..." (Al 'Imran 3:19)

"If anyone desires a religion other than Islam (submission to Allah), never will it be accepted of him..." (Al 'Imran 3:85)

"Do they seek for other than the Religion of Allah? - while all creatures of the heavens and on earth have, willing or unwilling, bowed to His Will (accepted Islam)..." (Al 'Imran 3:83)

The submission (Islam) of all living things, willing or otherwise, is mentioned because all created things are enslaved to Allah in general terms, whether they acknowledge it or not. They are all submitted to Him and are controlled by Him, and so they are *"muslim"* whether they submit willingly or unwillingly. No living creature can operate outside His Will and Decree, and there is no strength and no power except in Him. He is the Lord and Controller of the Worlds, directing them as He wills. He is the Creator, Originator and Designer of all, and everything apart from Him is subject to Him, created and formed by Him, in need of Him, enslaved and dominated by Him. He, may He be glorified, is the One *(al-Wahid)*, the Subduer *(al-Qahhar)*, the Creator *(al-Khaliq)*, the Evolver *(al-Bari')* the Fashioner *(al-Musawwir)*.

Allah the Creator

Although He may create things through certain means, He is still the Creator, the One Who decrees what should be. So the means depends on Allah just as man does. There is nothing in the realm of created things that can operate independently of Allah, or cause good or harm unless He wills it. Every means requires another means with which to work, and it needs protection from its opposite which may cancel it out and prevent it from doing its job.

Allah is the only One Who has no need of anything else. He has no partner with whom He must work, and no opposite whom He must resist and oppose. He says:

"...Say: 'See you then? The things that you invoke besides Allah - can they, if Allah wills some Penalty for me, remove His Penalty? - or if He wills some Grace for me, can they keep back His Grace?' Say: 'Sufficient is Allah for me! In Him trust those who put their trust.'" (al-Zumar 39:38)

"If Allah touch you with affliction, none can remove it but He; if He touch you with happiness, He has power over all things." (al-An'am 6:17)

"[Ibrahim said:] ... 'O my people! I am indeed free from your (guilt) of giving partners to Allah. For me, I have set my face, firmly and truly, towards Him Who created the heavens and the earth, and never shall I give partners to Allah.' His people disputed with him. He said: '(Come) you to dispute with me, about Allah, when He (Himself) has guided me? I fear not (the beings)

you associate with Allah: unless my Lord wills, (nothing can happen)... It is those who believe and confuse not their beliefs with wrong - that are (truly) in security, for they are on (right) guidance." (al-An'am 6:78–80, 82)

Shirk and wrongdoing

In *al-Sahihayn* it is reported from 'Abdullah ibn Mas'ud 🌸 that when this *ayah* was revealed, the Companions of the Prophet 🌸 found it difficult. They said, "O Messenger of Allah! Which of us does not confuse his belief with wrong?" He said, "No, that refers to shirk. Have you not heard the words of the righteous slave: *'false worship [shirk] is indeed the highest wrongdoing'*?"

Ibrahim 🌸: Imam of *Tawhid*

When Ibrahim 🌸, the *Khalil* (close friend of Allah) and *imam* of the sincere *hanifs* was sent as a Prophet, the earth was filled with the religion of the *mushrikin*. Allah said:

"And remember that Ibrahim was tried by his Lord with certain Commands, which he fulfilled: He said: 'I will make you an Imam to the Nations.' He pleaded: 'And also (imams) from my offspring!' He answered: 'But My Promise is not within the reach of evildoers.'" (al-Baqarah 2:124)

Allah explained that this covenant of leadership (being an *imam*) does not extend to evildoers (*zalim*), for Allah does not say that an evildoer may be an *imam*; and the worst of evil (*zulm*) is shirk. Allah says:

"Ibrahim was indeed a model (ummah), devoutly obedient to Allah, (and) true in faith, and he joined not gods with Allah." (al-Nahl 16:120)

Ummah (here translated as "model") means a teacher of good who is taken as an example to follow.

Allah bestowed Prophethood and the Book upon his progeny, and the Prophets sent after him were sent in his footsteps with the same message. Allah says:

"So We have taught you the inspired (message), 'Follow the ways of Ibrahim the True in Faith, and he joined not gods with Allah.'" (al-Nahl 16:123)

"Without a doubt, among men, the nearest of kin to Ibrahim, are those who follow him, as are also this Prophet and those who believe: and Allah is the Protector of those who have Faith." (Al 'Imran 3:68)

"Ibrahim was not a Jew nor yet a Christian; but he was true in Faith, and bowed his will to Allah's, (which is Islam), and he joined not gods with Allah." (Al 'Imran 3:67)

"They say: 'Become Jews or Christians if you would be guided (to salvation).' Say: 'Nay! (I would rather) the Religion of Ibrahim, the True, and he joined not gods with Allah.' Say: 'We believe in Allah, and the revelation given to us, and to Ibrahim, Isma'il, Ishaq, Ya 'qub, and the Tribes, and that given to Musa and 'Isa, and that given to (all) Prophets from their Lord: we make no difference between one and another of them: and we bow to Allah (in Islam).'" (al-Baqarah 2:135–136)

It was reported in *al-Sahih* that the Prophet ﷺ said, "Ibrahim was the best of mankind" *(Muslim)*. Ibrahim ﷺ is the best of the Prophets after Prophet Muhammad ﷺ, and he is the *Khalil* (close friend) of Allah.

Khalil of Allah

It was also reported in *al-Sahih*, through another *isnad*, that the Prophet ﷺ said, "Allah has taken me as a *khalil* just as He took Ibrahim as a *khalil"* *(Muslim)*. He ﷺ also said, "If I were to take any of the people of this world as a *khalil*, I would have taken Abu Bakr as a *khalil*, but your companion [meaning himself] is the *khalil* of Allah" (Agreed upon). And he ﷺ said, "Do not leave any private entrance to the mosque without sealing it up, except the private entrance of Abu Bakr." He ﷺ also said:

"Indeed, among the people who came before you were some who took graves as places of worship. Do not take graves as places of worship, for I forbid you to do so." *(Muslim)*

All of this is reported in *al-Sahih*, and it is reported that he said these things a few days before his death, so they were the final touches to his message. This was the realisation of his close friendship (being *khalil*) with Allah, which was based on the love of Allah toward the slave and the love of the slave toward Allah - unlike the view of the *Jahamiyyah*.

This is also a realisation of the meaning of *Tawhid*, the Oneness of Allah, telling them that they should not worship anything except Him, and rejecting the ideas of those who are similar to the *mushrikin*. It is also a refutation of the *Rafidah* who seek to undermine the position of al-Siddiq [Abu Bakr] ﷺ, and who are the worst of those who claim to be Muslims because of their *shirk* and worship of 'Ali ﷺ and other human beings.

Khillah (close friendship) and *mahabbah* (love)

Khillah (being a *khalil*) is the perfection of the love *(mahabbah)* that is required of the slave in his position of total servitude to Allah and, with regard to Allah, it is the perfection of His divinity and position as *Rabb* over His slaves whom He loves and who love Him.

The word *'ubudiyyah* includes total humility and total love. This is what was attained - perfectly - by Ibrahim ﷺ and by Muhammad ﷺ.

For this reason the Prophet ﷺ did not have a *khalil* among the people of this world, because *khillah* cannot be divided, unlike the idea of *mahabbah* (love). In a *sahih hadith*, the Prophet 鬆 said of al-Hasan and Usamah, "O Allah, I love them so love them, and love those who love them." 'Amr ibn al-'As asked him, "Which of the people is most beloved to you?" He said, "'A'ishah". He asked, "Who among the men?" He said, "Her father". And the Prophet 鬆 said to 'Ali 鬆, "Tomorrow I shall give the banner to a man who loves Allah and His Messenger, and Allah and His Messenger love him" *(Agreed upon)*. And there are many other such examples.

What kind of people does Allah love?

Allah tells us:

"...Allah loves those who act aright." (Al 'Imran 3:76)

"...Allah loves those who do good (or are kind)." (al-Baqarah 2:195; al-Ma'idah 5:13)

"...Allah loves those who are fair (and just)." (al-Hujurat 49:9; al-Mumtahinah 60:8)

"...Allah loves those who turn to Him constantly and He loves those who keep themselves pure and clean." (al-Baqarah 2:222)

"Truly Allah loves those who fight in His cause in battle array, as if they were a solid cemented structure." (al-Saff 61:4)

"...Soon will Allah produce a people whom He will love as they will love Him..." (al-Ma'idah 5:54)

Allah has told us how He loves His believing slaves, and how they love Him:

"...those of Faith are overflowing in their love for Allah..." (al-Baqarah 2:165)

But *khillah,* unlike *mahabbah,* is something rare and special, reserved for the few. Some people say that Muhammad ﷺ is the *habib* (beloved) of Allah and Ibrahim ﷺ is the *khalil* (close friend) of Allah, thinking that *mahabbah* is of a higher status than *khillah,* but this is incorrect, for Muhammad ﷺ is also the *khalil* of Allah, as is proven in numerous *sahih ahadith.*

Complete love for Allah

We have already stated above that loving Allah means loving Him and loving that which He loves, as it was reported in *al-Sahihayn* that the Prophet ﷺ said:

> "There are three things, whoever has them has discovered the sweetness of faith: when Allah and His Messenger are more beloved to him than anyone else, when he loves another only for the sake of Allah, and when he would hate to return to *kufr* after Allah has saved him from it just as he would hate to be thrown into fire." *(Al-Bukhari and Muslim)*

The Prophet ﷺ explained that whoever attains these three qualities has discovered the sweetness of faith, because finding sweetness in something comes as a result of loving it. Whoever loves or desires a thing, when he attains what he desires, will find sweetness, joy and happiness in it.

The perfection of love is that Allah and His Messenger become more beloved to a person than everything else, for when it comes to love of Allah and His Messenger, it is not enough to have just a little love; Allah and His Messenger must be dearer than all else, as explained above.

The sign of this is that when he loves a person, he loves him only for the sake of Allah. And in order to avoid anything that could undermine this, he hates everything that is opposed to faith as he would hate to be thrown into fire.

So loving the Messenger and the believers is part of loving Allah, and the Messenger of Allah ﷺ loves the believers whom Allah loves, because he is the most perfect of mankind in loving for the sake of Allah and in loving what Allah loves and hating what Allah hates. There is no share in *khillah* for anyone or anything other than Allah, as he ﷺ said, "If I were to take any of the people of this world as a *khalil,* I would have taken Abu Bakr as a *khalil*" *(Agreed upon).* From this we know that *khillah* is of a higher status than *mahabbah.*

What is meant is that both *khillah* and *mahabbah* of Allah are realisations of *'ubudiyyah.* The one who thinks that *'ubudiyyah* is a matter only of humility and submission, with no love, and that love is a matter of whims or pampering which do not befit the divine Lord, is making a great mistake. Hence it was reported from Dhu'1-Nun that when people started to discuss the issue of *mahabbah* with him, he said, "Stop talking about this matter, otherwise some people might think that they have achieved that!"

Too much talk about love?

Some of the scholars expressed their disapproval of gatherings in which people talk too much about love without having the proper fear of Allah.

One of the *Salaf* said, "Whoever worships Allah on the basis of love only is a *zindiq,* and whoever worships him on the basis of hope only is a *murji',* and whoever worships Him on the basis of fear only is a *haruri,* but whoever worships Him on the basis of love and fear and hope is a monotheistic believer." So we see among some of the later generations those who talk too much and too freely about *mahabbah,* to the extent that it has led them into misbehaviour and false claims that contradict true *'ubudiyyah,* and make a person claim to have attributes that befit none save Allah. They may even claim things that are beyond the reach of the Prophets and Messengers, or they may ask Allah for things that do not befit anyone, not even the Prophets and Messengers, in any way, and are appropriate only for Allah.

This is a trap into which many *shaykhs* have fallen, and the reason for it is their failure to attain the true *'ubudiyyah* which the Messengers reached and which is detailed in the commands and prohibitions which they brought. It is due to a weak understanding of the true nature of *'ubudiyyah,* for if a person's understanding is weak and he has little knowledge of Islam, and he also has strong but unfocused love in his heart, he may say foolish things as a result, just as a person who is foolish and ignorant may be inappropriately informal in his love for another, so that he says things that make his beloved angry or annoyed, or may even make him punish him.

There are many who, in their claims of loving Allah, do things that show ignorance of Islam, such as transgressing the limits set by Allah, neglecting their duties towards Allah, or making false claims that have no basis in reality, such as, "Any follower of mine who leaves anybody in Hell, I disown him", or, "Any follower of mine who leaves any of the believers behind who has entered Hell, I disown him."

In the first case, this *shaykh* is saying that his followers have the power to bring everyone out of Hell, and in the second case he is saying that his followers have the power to prevent people who are guilty of major sins from entering Hell.

One of them said, "On the Day of Resurrection I will set up my tent over Hell so that no-one will enter it."

Such sayings have been reported from some of the well-known *shaykhs.* Either they are lies that are falsely attributed to them, or they are mistakes on their part.

Such words may be uttered in a trance or state of oblivion *(fana')* when a person no longer knows what he is saying or doing. This state of trance is a state of joy without discretion, which is why when these people wake up from that trance, they seek forgiveness for what they have said. Those *shaykhs* who go to extremes in listening to *qasidahs* that speak of love, longing, yearning and so on, take these emotions as their aim, for this kind of *qasidah* provokes any kind of love in the heart. Allah has revealed the standard against which their love may be tested. He says:

> *"Say: 'If you do love Allah, follow me [i.e. the Prophet ﷺ]: Allah will love you...'"* (Al 'Imran 3:31)

One cannot truly love Allah without following His Messenger, and one cannot truly follow and obey the Messenger without being a true slave of Allah *('ubudiyyah)*. Many of those who claim to love Allah transgress His *shari'ah* and ignore the Sunnah of His Prophet ﷺ, and make many claims that cannot be discussed here. Some of them may even think that they are no longer obliged to do *fard* acts, or that they are permitted to do *haram* things, and other things which go against the law and Sunnah of the Prophet ﷺ.

Love = *Jihad*

Allah has made the basis of love for Him and His Messenger *jihad* for His sake. *Jihad* involves absolute love for that which Allah has commanded, and absolute hatred for that which He has forbidden, and so He has described those whom He loves and who love Him as:

> *"...lowly with the Believers, mighty against the Rejecters, fighting in the Way of Allah and never afraid of the reproaches of such as find fault."* (al-Ma'idah 5:54)

Hence the love of this *ummah* for Allah is more perfect than the love of the nations that came before, and their servitude *('ubudiyyah)* towards

Him is more perfect than the servitude of the nations who came before. The most perfect of this *ummah* in this regard are the Companions of Muhammad ﷺ, so whoever is more like them is also more perfect. But do we see any of this in those who claim to love Allah?

Some *shaykhs* say that love is a fire which destroys anything in the heart other than what the Beloved (Allah) wants, and they mean that everything that happens is what Allah wants to happen. They think that the perfection of love is when a man loves everything, even *kufr* and immorality and sin! But nobody can love absolutely everything; man only loves that which suits him and is for his own benefit, and he hates that which goes against him and harms him. But what they want when they mention these misleading ideas is to follow their own whims and desires, so that they can indulge in their own whims even more. So they love the things they desire, such as images, power, wealth and misguided innovations, claiming that this is part of loving Allah. But whoever truly loves Allah hates what Allah and His Messenger hate, and strives against it with his own soul and his wealth.

Universal vs. legislative will of Allah

The reason for their error is that when they describe love as a fire that burns everything in the heart except what the Beloved (meaning Allah) desires, they mistakenly refer to the universal will of Allah which is manifested in everything that exists.

But when the one who believes in Allah and in His Books and Messengers says this, he means the legislative, religious will of Allah, which affects that which Allah loves and which pleases Him, so if he says that love burns away everything in the heart except that which is beloved by Allah, then this is correct, for perfect love of Allah means that one only loves that which Allah loves. So if a person loves something that Allah does not love, it means that his love is imperfect. Although Allah decrees that *kufr* and sin should exist, He loathes and hates these things, and forbids them. If I do not also hate what He hates and despises, then I do not truly love Him, but I love what He hates.

Loving Allah – a universal principle

Following this *shari'ah* and engaging in *jihad* for its sake are some of the greatest differences between those who truly love Allah and His friends *(awliya')* whom He loves and who love Him, and those who claim to love Allah but focus on the idea of Him being the Lord of everyone, Muslim and *kafir* alike, or who follow some of the misguided innovations that go against His law. This claim of loving Allah is like that of the Jews and Christians, if not even worse than the claim of the Jews and the Christians, because of the elements of hypocrisy that it contains, and it is known that the hypocrites will be in the lowest level of Hell.

The *Tawrat* (Torah) and *Injil* (Gospel) encourage love for Allah, and they are all agreed on this. Indeed, in their religion it is believed to be one of the greatest commandments brought by al-Namus (Jibril ﷺ).

In the Gospel, the greatest commandment given by the Messiah is, "That you should love Allah with all your heart and with all your mind and with all your soul." The Christians claim to love Allah in this manner, and that the asceticism and other forms of worship that they practise are signs of that. But in fact they have nothing to do with loving Allah, for they do not follow that which He loves; in fact they follow that which He hates, and they despise that which pleases Him, so their deeds are to no avail.

Drawing close to Allah through *wajib* and *mustahabb* deeds

Allah hates and curses the *kafirs,* and He loves those who love Him. It is impossible for a person to love Allah without Allah loving him in turn; as much as a slave loves His Lord, Allah loves him, and indeed the reward that Allah gives His slave is greater than that, as is reported in the *sahih hadith qudsi* in which we are told that Allah says:

> "...If he draws near to Me a hand's span, I draw near to him an arm's length; and if he draws near to Me an arm's length, I draw near to him a fathom's length. And if he comes to Me walking, I go to him at speed." *(Al-Bukhari and Muslim)*

Allah tells us that He loves the pious who fear Him, those who do good, those who are patient, those who turn to Him in repentance and those who purify themselves. He loves those who do the things that He commands, whether *wajib* or *mustahabb,* as is mentioned in the *sahih hadith*:

> "My slave will keep drawing near to Me with supererogatory deeds until I love him, and when I love him I will be his hearing with which he hears, his sight with which he sees..." *(Al-Bukhari)*

Many of those who follow errors in areas such as asceticism *(zuhd)* and worship fall into the same trap as the Christians, by claiming to love Allah whilst doing things that go against His law, by not striving in *jihad* for His sake, and so on. They adhere to religious practices which they hope will bring them closer to Allah but which are like those which the Christians adhered to on the basis of ambiguous texts, or stories whose narrators were not trustworthy, or who even if they were trustworthy were not infallible, so they began to innovate a way for their followers, just as the Christian monks and priests innovated a way for their followers. Then they fell short with regard to *'ubudiyyah,* claiming that the "elite" are exempted in part, just as the Christians claim with regard to the Messiah and their priests. They affirm that their "elite" have attributes in common with Allah, just as the Christians say about the Messiah, his mother and their priests and monks.

True religion is the realisation of servitude to Allah in all aspects, which means truly loving Allah on all levels. The more perfect the slave's servitude towards Allah is, the more perfect his love for his Lord is, and the Lord's love for His slave. The more lacking the former is, the more lacking the latter is. The more a person has love in his heart for anything other than Allah, the more enslaved he is to something other than Allah, and the more enslaved he is to something other than Allah, the more love he has for something other than Allah.

All love that is not for Allah is false and worthless, and every deed that is not done for the sake of Allah is false and worthless. This world and all that is in it is cursed, except that which is done for the sake of Allah, and it cannot be for the sake of Allah unless it is something which Allah and His Messenger love, which is what is prescribed by Islam.

Every deed which is done for the sake of something other than Allah cannot be for the sake of Allah, and every deed which is not in accordance with the religion of Allah cannot be for the sake of Allah. Nothing can be for the sake of Allah unless it meets both of two conditions: it should be for the sake of Allah, and it should be in accordance with that which Allah and His Messenger love. This is what is *wajib* and *mustahabb,* as Allah says:

> *"...whoever expects to meet his Lord, let him work righteousness, and in the worship of his Lord, admit no-one as partner."* (al-Kahf 18:110)

Righteous deeds are essential, namely *wajib* and *mustahabb* deeds, and they must be done purely for the sake of Allah, as Allah says:

> *"Nay - whoever submits his whole self to Allah and is a doer of good - he will get his reward with his Lord: on such shall be no fear, nor shall they grieve."* (al-Baqarah 2:112)

Actions, intentions and *shirk*

The Prophet ﷺ said:

"Whoever does a deed that is not part of this matter of ours [i.e. Islam] will have it rejected." *(Ahmad and Muslim)*

And he said:

"Actions are but by intention and every man shall have but that which he intended. Thus he whose migration was for Allah and His Messenger, his migration was for Allah and His Messenger, and he whose migration was for some worldly benefit or to take some woman in marriage, his migration was for that for which he migrated." *(Al-Bukhari and Muslim)*

This principle is the basis of Islam; true religion is realised in accordance with the realisation of this principle. This is the principle with which Allah sent the Messengers and revealed His Books. It is the principle to which the Messenger called and for which he fought and strove; it is what he commanded and encouraged, and it is the central pivot around which the entire religion revolves.

Shirk is overwhelmingly common among people, as it says in the *hadith*: "In this *ummah* it is more subtle than the noise made by the footsteps of an ant" *(Al-Tabarani)*. According to another *hadith*, Abu Bakr ﷺ said, "O Messenger of Allah, how can we be saved from it when it is more subtle than the noise made by the footsteps of an ant?" The Prophet ﷺ said to Abu Bakr:

"I shall teach you a word which, if you say it, will protect you from *shirk*, major and minor. Say: 'O Allah, I seek refuge with You from associating anything with You knowingly, and I seek Your forgiveness for that of which I am unaware." *(Abu Ya'la)*

'Umar ﷺ used to say in his *du'a'*, "O Allah, make all my deeds righteous and make them purely for Your sake, and do not let there be any share for anyone else (in my intention)."

Much of that which people mix with their intentions when doing things is their hidden desires, which prevent them from achieving true love of Allah, or true servitude and sincerity toward Him. Shaddad ibn Aws said, "O Arabs, O Arabs! The thing I fear most for you is showing off and hidden desires." It was said to Abu Dawud al-Sajistani, "What is the hidden desire?" He said, "Love of leadership."

Ka'b ibn Malik reported that the Prophet ﷺ said:
> "Two hungry wolves sent against the sheepfold will not do more damage to it than a man's eagerness for wealth and prestige does to his religion." *(Ahmad, al-Tirmidhi and Abu Ya'la)*
> Al-Tirmidhi said it is a *sahih hasan hadith*.

The Prophet ﷺ was explaining that the damage done to a person's religion by his eagerness for wealth and prestige is no less than the damage done by two hungry wolves to the flock of sheep. This is quite obvious, for if a man's religion is sound, he will not have any eagerness for those things. Once the heart has tasted the sweetness of true servitude to Allah and love for Him, nothing else will be dearer to him than that and nothing else will take priority. Thus evil and shameful deeds are turned away from those who are sincere towards Allah, as Allah says:
> *"...thus (did We order) that We might turn away from him (all) evil and shameful deeds: for he was one of Our slaves, sincere and purified."*
> (Yusuf 12:24)

Sincerity towards Allah

The one who is sincere towards Allah has tasted the sweetness of true servitude toward Him, which keeps him from becoming enslaved by anything else, and he has tasted the sweetness of loving Allah, which keeps him from loving anything else. For the sound heart, there is nothing sweeter or more delightful than the sweetness of faith which includes servitude to, love for and sincerity towards Allah. This means that the heart is attracted towards Allah, turning to Him, fearing Him and putting its hope in Him, as Allah says:

"Who feared (Allah) Most Gracious unseen, and brought a heart turned in devotion (to Him)." (Qaf 50:33)

The one who loves, fears losing the thing he is seeking, or getting the thing he dreads, so the slave of Allah who loves Him must always be between hope and fear, as Allah says:

"Those whom they call upon do desire (for themselves) means of access to their Lord - even those who are nearest: they hope for His mercy and fear His Wrath, for the Wrath of your Lord is something to take heed of." (al-Isra' 17:57)

If the slave is sincere towards Allah, He will choose him, revive his heart and bring him close to Him, and will turn away from him all evil and shameful deeds that contradict that. He fears attaining the opposite of that, unlike the heart that is not sincere towards Allah, which has a will and is seeking for something to love, although this love is not focused and may fall in love with anything he comes across and happens to desire. The heart is like the branch of a tree which may be swayed and bent by any passing breeze, so sometimes the heart may be attracted to images, forbidden or otherwise, and so it remains a prisoner, enslaved by something which, if it had become a slave to him, it would have been something to be ashamed of.

Enslavement to money and power

Sometimes the heart is attracted by prestige and power, so a mere word may make it happy or angry, and it is enslaved by the one who praises it even if that praise is false, whilst it is hostile towards the one who criticises it even if the criticism is well-founded.

Sometimes the heart is enslaved by the *dirham* and *dinar*, and other things by which hearts may be enslaved because of their desire for them, and so it takes its desire as a god, and follows its desires instead of following the guidance of Allah.

If a person is not sincere towards Allah and does not become His slave, so that his heart is enslaved by his Lord alone, with no partner or associate, and Allah is dearer to him than all else, and he is humble and submissive towards Him, he will be enslaved by created beings and the *shayatin* will dominate his heart, so he will be one of the misguided brothers of the *shayatin* and will be overwhelmed by evil and shameful deeds, the extent of which Allah alone knows.

This is the way it is; there can be no other way.

True belief

If the heart is not true in faith towards Allah, turning only to Him and turning away from all else, then a person is a *mushrik*:

> "So set your face steadily and truly to the Faith: (establish) Allah's
> handiwork according to the pattern on which He has made mankind:
> no change (let there be) in the work (wrought) by Allah: that is the
> Standard Religion: but most among mankind understand not. Turn back
> in repentance to Him, and fear Him: establish regular prayers, and be
> not among those who join gods with Allah — Those who split up their

Religion, and become (mere) Sects — each party rejoicing in that which is with itself!" (al-Rum 30:30-32)

Ibrahim ﷺ and Pharaoh: contrasting families

Allah has made Ibrahim ﷺ and the family of Ibrahim ﷺ leaders and examples of those true believers who truly love and worship Allah in all sincerity, and He has made Pharaoh and the family of Pharaoh leaders and examples of the *mushrikin* who follow their own desires. Allah says about Ibrahim ﷺ:

"And We bestowed on him Ishaq and, as an additional gift, (a grandson), Ya'qub, and We made righteous men of every one (of them). And We made them leaders, guiding (men) by Our Command, and We sent them inspiration to do good deeds, to establish regular prayers, and to practise regular charity; and they constantly served Us (and Us only)." (al-Anbiya' 21:72-73)

Concerning Pharaoh and his people, Allah says:

"And We made them (but) leaders inviting to the Fire: and on the Day of Judgement no help shall they find. In this world We made a Curse to follow them: and on the Day of Judgement they will be among the loathed (and despised)." (al-Qasas 28:41-42)

Hence at first the followers of Pharaoh were unable to distinguish between what Allah loves and approves of and what He decrees and wills to happen, thinking only in terms of the comprehensive will of Allah, then in the end they were unable to distinguish between the Creator and His creation, and thought that they were one and the same.

Their prominent figures think that *shari'ah* involves both obedience and sin, *haqiqah* involves sin without obedience, and *tahqiq* involves obedience without sin. This *tahqiq* is the way of Pharaoh and his people, who denied the Creator and denied that Allah spoke to His slave Musa ﷺ and sent him with commands and prohibitions.

Al-'Ubudiyyah

Part Four

"'Do you then see whom you have been worshipping - you and your fathers before you? - for they are enemies to me; not so the Lord and Cherisher of the Worlds'."

(al-Shu'ara' 26:75-77)

The difference between the Creator and His creation

Ibrahim ﷺ and his believing family, i.e. the Prophets and those who believed in them, knew that there had to be a difference between the Creator and His creation, and between obedience and sin. The more the slave realises this difference, the more he increases in love for and servitude towards Allah, so he turns further away from worshipping, loving and obeying anything except Allah. Those misguided *mushrikin*, on the other hand, view Allah and His creation as equal. Ibrahim ﷺ said:

> "'Do you then see whom you have been worshipping - you and your fathers before you? - for they are enemies to me; not so the Lord and Cherisher of the Worlds'." (al-Shu'ara' 26:75-77)

But they use as evidence the ambiguous words of their *shaykhs,* just as the Christians did with the words of their priests.

Fana' ("oblivion")

An example of this is the concept of *fana'* (extinction of individual consciousness, recedence of the ego, obliteration of the self). *Fana'* is of three types:
1. The *fana'* of the Prophets and *awliya'* who have attained perfection.
2. The *fana'* of the *awliya'* and righteous people who are striving in the right direction even though they are not perfect.
3. The *fana'* of the hypocrites and heretics who liken Allah to His creation.

The first type of *fana'* means the obliteration of the desire for anything except Allah, so that a person does not love anyone or anything except Allah, he does not worship anything except Him, he does not rely on anyone except Him, and he does not ask from anyone except Him.

This is the sense which should be understood from the words of Shaykh Abu Yazid: "I want not to want anything except what He wants, what pleases the Beloved [i.e. Allah]." This is what is meant by the religious will of Allah. Perfection means that a man does not want, love or like anything except what Allah wants, loves and likes, which is what He has commanded and made *wajib* or *mustahabb*. He only loves those whom Allah loves, such as the angels, Prophets and righteous people. This is what is meant by their interpretation of the *ayah*, *"But only he (will prosper) who brings to Allah a sound heart"* (al-Shu'ara' 26:89). They said it is sound and safe from everything except being a slave to Allah, or everything except wanting what Allah wants, or everything except loving Allah. The meaning is the same and whether it is called *fana'* or not, it is the beginning and end of Islam, the focus of the entire religion.

The second type of *fana'* is oblivion towards others, which is attained by many of those who follow the path, because their hearts are strongly attracted to remembering, worshipping and loving Allah, and distracted from noticing anyone or anything else. Nothing crosses their minds except thoughts of Allah; they are not even aware of anything else, as was said in the interpretation of the *ayah*, *"But there came to be a void in the heart of the mother of Musa: she was going almost to disclose his (case), had We not strengthened her heart (with faith)..."* (al-Qasas 28:10). They said her heart was oblivious to everything except thoughts of Musa, which is the kind of thing that often happens to those who are overwhelmed with some concern, whether it be love or hope or fear – the heart is distracted from everything except that which is loved or hoped for or feared, so that it is unaware of anything else.

If this kind of *fana'* overwhelms a person, his focus on Allah becomes so intense that he is no longer aware of anything else, not his own existence or the *dhikr* he is doing, and everything diminishes in his senses, every created being, the person himself and everyone else, and there remains only the Lord. What is meant is that everything is diminished in a person's perception, so that he no longer notices or remembers anything, and is quite oblivious to what is going on around him. If this feeling becomes so strong that the person becomes confused and can no longer make proper distinctions, he may think that he is his beloved, as it was said that a man fell into the water, and the one who loved him threw himself in after him. The former said, "I fell in by accident; what made you fall?" and the latter replied, "I was so overwhelmed with love for you that I thought I was you."

This idea has caused many people to stumble, so that they thought in terms of physical unity whereby there is no longer any difference between a person and the object of his love. This is incorrect, for the Creator cannot be united with anything at all. Indeed, nothing can be totally united with anything else without becoming something else altogether; the essence of the two things is lost when they unite, and they become a third thing, neither this nor that, as is the case when water and milk are mixed together, or water and wine, and so on. But what is loved and wanted by both becomes one, and what is hated and loathed by both becomes one, so they love and hate the same things. One loves what the other loves, hates what the other hates, befriends those whom the other befriends and takes as enemies those whom the other takes as enemies. This kind of *fana'* is far from perfect.

The greatest *awliya'*, like Abu Bakr 🙵 and 'Umar 🙵, and the earliest *muhajirun* and *ansar* - let alone the Prophets who are above them in status – did not experience this kind of *fana'*. This emerged after the time of the *Sahabah*.

The *Sahabah* never experienced this type of *fana'* or any loss of their faculties because of the strength of *iman* in their hearts. The *Sahabah*, may Allah be pleased with them, were too strong and firm in their faith to lose their minds in this fashion, or to experience any kind of swooning, loss of consciousness, intoxication, oblivion, rapture or ecstasy.

These things began to emerge at the time of the *Tabi'in,* among the worshippers of al-Basrah, among whom were some who would swoon or even die when they heard the Qur'an, such as Abu Juhayr al-Darir and Zararah ibn Awfa, the *qadi* (judge) of al-Basrah.

Some of the Sufi *shaykhs* experience a kind of oblivion and intoxication where they are unable to make proper distinctions, and when they are in that state they may say words which, when they come round, they realise are wrong. Such stories are reported about (ascetics such as) Abu Yazid, Abu'l-Hasan al-Nuri and Abu Bakr al-Shibli, and so on, unlike Abu Sulayman al-Darini, Ma'ruf al-Karkhi, and al-Fudayl ibn 'Ayyad, let alone al-Junayd and so on, who remained of sound mind throughout all their experiences and who never fell into states of oblivion or intoxication, etc. Those who have reached a level of perfection have nothing in their hearts except love for Allah and the desire to worship Him alone. They have vast knowledge and proper discretion, so they see things as they really are, and they see that created beings exist only by the command of Allah, and are controlled by Him, submitting to His will and turning to Him. This increases their faith and insight, and whatever they see of His creation supports and enhances the sincerity and submission of their hearts, and reinforces their belief in *Tawhid* and their worship of Him alone, with no partners or associates.

This is the reality to which the Qur'an calls. This is the basis of the perfect faith of those who truly know Allah, of whom our Prophet ﷺ is the leader and most perfect. Hence when he was taken up into the heavens (the *mi'raj),* and saw the signs and wonders that he saw, and received Revelation there, the next morning no trace of his experience could be seen on him, and he did not look any different, unlike Musa ﷺ who had lost consciousness (when he spoke with Allah).

The third type, which may be called *fana',* is where a person affirms that nothing exists except Allah, and that the existence of the Creator and the existence of His creation are one and the same, so there is no difference between the Lord and the slave. This is the *fana'* of misguided heretics who think that Allah is part of the universe. This idea was disowned by the *shaykhs,* one of whom said, "I do not see anything except Allah", or "I do not look at anything except Allah", and so on. What was meant was: I do not see any Lord except Allah, or any Creator or Controller except Him, or any God except Him, and I do not look to anyone but Him with love and fear and hope; for the eye looks towards that to which the heart is attached. Whoever loves a thing, or has hope in it or fears it, will turn towards it. If there is no love for it in the heart, or hope or fear or hatred, or any other emotion that ties the heart to it, then the heart will not turn deliberately towards it or look towards it. If it accidentally glances at it, it will be like a man who happens to glance at a wall or anything else that means nothing to him.

The righteous *shaykhs,* may Allah be pleased with them, mentioned something about true *Tawhid* and sincere submission, whereby the slave does not turn to anything except Allah and does not look at anything other than Him, whether with love, fear or hope; the heart is empty of every created being and does not look at them except with the light of Allah.

So he hears with the Truth, sees with the Truth, strikes with the Truth and walks with the Truth. He loves that which Allah loves and hates that which Allah hates; he takes as friends those whom Allah takes as friends, and regards as enemies those whom Allah regards as enemies. He fears Allah with regard to His creation, but he does not fear created beings with regard to his duties towards Allah. He places his hope in Allah with regard to His creation, but he does not place his hope in created beings with regard to his duties towards Allah. This is the sound, believing Muslim heart, which has perfect faith in Allah alone and truly understands the message of the Prophets and Messengers.

This third type of *fana'*, which believes that Allah is what one can see (pantheism), is the idea, belief and *"tawhid"* of the people of Pharaoh, and of other similar types such as the *Qaramitah* (Karmathians) and so on.

On the other hand, the kind of *fana'* experienced by the followers of the Prophets is the praiseworthy kind of *fana'*, and the one who experiences it is one of those whom Allah praised by calling them His pious friends (*awliya'*), successful supporters and victorious troops.

These *shaykhs* and righteous people did not mean, "what I see of created beings is the Lord of heaven and earth". No one would say such a thing except those who are totally misguided and corrupt, whether the fault is in their way of thinking or in their beliefs. Such people are in a state between madness and heresy.

All the trustworthy *shaykhs* agree with the consensus of the early generations and *imams* of this *ummah*, which is that the Creator, may He be glorified, is distinct from His creation; there is nothing of His essence in His creation, and nothing of His creation in His essence. It is essential to distinguish the Ancient and Eternal One Who has no beginning from the finite event of existence, and to distinguish the Creator from His creation. The *shaykhs* have said much more on this topic than we can discuss here.

They have spoken about the diseases and doubts that may affect people's hearts and minds. Someone may see creation, and think that it is the Creator of heaven and earth, because he cannot distinguish between them in his mind. This is like the one who sees a ray of sunlight and imagines that this is the sun itself.

Al-'Ubudiyyah

Part Five

"Nay - whoever submits his whole self to Allah and is a doer of good - he will get his reward with his Lord: on such shall be no fear nor shall they grieve."

(al-Baqarah 2:112)

Worship of Allah Alone, as He prescribed

The entire religion is based on two things:
That we should not worship anything except Allah, and that we should not worship Him except in the manner that He has prescribed in *shari'ah*, and that we should not worship Him by means of *bid'ah* (reprehensible innovations). As Allah says:

> "...whoever expects to meet his Lord, let him work righteousness, and, in the worship of his Lord, admit no one as partner." (al-Kahf 18:110)

This is the realisation of the *shahadatayn*, the witness that there is no god except Allah, and that Muhammad is the Messenger of Allah. The first part tells us that we should worship none but Him, and the second part tells us that Muhammad is His Messenger who conveyed the Message from Him, so we must believe what he has told us and obey what he has told us to do.

The Prophet 鑾 has explained how we should worship Allah, and has forbidden us from doing newly invented things, which he has told us are a going-astray. Allah says:

> "Nay - whoever submits his whole self to Allah and is a doer of good - he will get his reward with his Lord: on such shall be no fear nor shall they grieve." (al-Baqarah 2:112)

Worship Allah and obey His Messenger

Just as we are commanded not to fear anything except Allah, not to put our trust in anything but Allah, not to turn to anything except Allah, not to seek the help of anything except Allah and not to worship anything except Allah, so we are also commanded to follow and obey the Messenger and to take him as our example. The *halal* is that which he has permitted and the *haram* is that which he has forbidden. The religion is that which he has prescribed. Allah says:

> *"If only they had been content with what Allah and His Messenger gave them, and had said, 'Sufficient unto us is Allah! Allah and His Messenger will soon give us of His bounty: to Allah do we turn our hopes!' (That would have been the right course)."* (al-Tawbah 9:59)

Allah and His Messenger are the point of reference:

> *"...So take what the Messenger assigns to you, and deny yourselves that which he withholds from you..."* (al-Hashr 59:7)

Putting our trust only in Allah

We should put our trust only in Allah:

> *"[If only they...] had said, 'Sufficient unto us is Allah!...'"* (al-Tawbah 9:59)

Here the Messenger is not mentioned. Elsewhere the *Sahabah* (may Allah be pleased with them) are described as:

> *"Men said to them: 'A great army is gathering against you, so fear them': but it (only) increased their faith; they said: 'For us Allah suffices, and he is the best Disposer of affairs.'"* (Al 'Imran 3:173)

> *"O Prophet! Sufficient unto you is Allah - (unto you) and unto those who follow you among the Believers."* (al-Anfal 8:64)

> *"Is not Allah enough for His slave?..."* (al-Zumar 39:36)

> *"...Allah and His Messenger will soon give us of His bounty..."* (al-Tawbah 9:59)

So the giving is attributed to both Allah and His Messenger, but the bounty *[fadl]* is Allah's alone, and it is mentioned first [in the original Arabic] because bounty is in the hand of Allah and He gives it to whom

He wills. Allah is the Lord of grace [or bounty - *fadl*] unbounded [*dhufadlin 'azim* - see al–Anfal 8:29].

Allah says:

"... '*To Allah do we turn our hopes!*'..." (al–Tawbah 9:59)

So hope should be placed in Allah alone, as Allah says:

"*Therefore, when you are free (from your immediate task), still labour hard, And to your Lord, turn (all) your attention.*" (al–Inshirah 94:7-8)

The Prophet ﷺ said to Ibn 'Abbas:

"If you ask, then ask from Allah, and if you seek help, seek help from Allah." (*Ahmad and al-Tirmidhi*)

The Qur'an also says the same thing in several places.
Worship, fear and piety are only for Allah, but obedience and love are for Allah and His Messenger. Nuh ﷺ said to his people, "'...*that you should worship Allah, fear Him and obey me*'" (Nuh 71:3).

Allah says:

"*It is such as obey Allah and His Messenger, and fear Allah and do right, that will win (in the end).*" (al-Nur 24:52)

Worshipping Allah Alone

The Messengers commanded people to worship Allah alone, to focus only on Him and to put their trust only in Him, but to obey Him and them. *Shaytan* led the Christians and others astray, so that they associated partners with Allah and disobeyed His Messenger. They took their priests and anchorites, and the Messiah son of Maryam, as lords instead of Allah, and started to turn to them and put their trust in them, asking them for things whilst disobeying their commandments and going against their examples. Allah guided the believers who are sincere towards Him, the followers of the Straight Path, who know the truth and follow it, so they are not those whose portion is wrath or those who go astray. So they submitted sincerely to Allah and turned to their Lord, loving Him, putting their hope in Him, fearing Him and asking from Him, focusing all their attention on Him and delegating all their affairs to Him, putting their trust in Him, and they obeyed and honoured His Messengers, taking them as their friends, following them and adhering to their teachings and guidance.

This is the religion of Islam, with which Allah sent all His Messengers, earlier and later alike. This is the only religion which Allah will accept, and it is true worship of the Lord of the Worlds.

We ask Allah Almighty to help us to be steadfast and perfect in following His religion, and to cause us and all our Muslim brothers to die in a state of Islam.

Praise be to Allah alone, and peace and blessings be upon our master Muhammad and his family and companions.

Glossary

ahl al-kalam:
> Islamic philosophers or theologians.

al-Sahihayn:
> the two books of *Sahih*, collections of authentic *ahadith* compiled by Al-Bukhari and Muslim.

Ansar:
> "Helpers", the Muslims of Madinah at the time of the Prophet ﷺ.

ayah (pl. *ayat*):
> literally, "sign"; a "verse" of the Qur'an.

bid'ah:
> reprehensible innovation, the introduction of rites or beliefs into Islam that have no basis in the Qur'an or Sunnah.

deen:
> religion, way of life.

dhikr:
> "remembrance" i.e. of Allah.

dinar:
> a coin, money (cf. Latin *denarius*).

dirham:
> a coin, money (cf. Latin *drachma*).

du'a':
> supplication, "private" or "informal" prayer, which may be in Arabic or one's own language.

fana':
> annihilation, obliteration of the self; based on the Qur'anic *ayah*, "Everyone on it will pass away" (55:26).

hadith qudsi:
> literally, "sacred *hadith*", a *hadith* containing words of Allah that were narrated by the Prophet ﷺ, but which do not form part of the Qur'an.

***hadith*: (pl. *ahadith*):**

a saying or tradition of the Prophet ﷺ.

***halal*:**

permissible, allowed.

***hanif* (pl. *hunafa'*):**

a monotheist who worshipped no god but Allah and adhered to the way of Ibrahim ﷺ, prior to the Prophethood of Muhammad ﷺ.

***haram*:**

forbidden, prohibited.

***'ibadah*:**

worship.

***Iblis*:**

see *Shaytan*.

***ijtihad*:**

creative self-exertion to derive laws from the legitimate sources.

***iman*:**

faith, belief.

***isnad*:**

"chain of authority", the chain of people who conveyed a *hadith* from the Prophet ﷺ. Scholars who specialised in *hadith,* such as Al-Bukhari and Muslim, subjected the *isnad* of each *hadith* they came across to intense scrutiny. Only if they were certain that each person in the *isnad* was competent and truthful, and that each had been in a position to meet and learn from or teach the next person in the chain, would the scholars accept a *hadith* as being authentic.

***Isra'*:**

the Night Journey of the Prophet ﷺ, when he was taken from Makkah to Jerusalem.

***Jabari*:**

a sect which denied the free will of man.

***Jahami, Jahamiyyah*:**

a sect which denied the attributes of Allah as mentioned in the Qur'an.

Jibril:

known in English as the Archangel Gabriel.

jihad:

literally, "struggle" or "striving". Although this word is often translated as "holy war", it has a broader meaning than of warfare on the battlefield. Any act of striving to please Allah may be described as *jihad*.

jinn:

created beings made from smokeless fire. In many ways they are a parallel creation to humans, as there are Muslims and *kafirs* among them, they are born, have children and die, etc. They can see us, but we cannot see them. Trying to see or contact them is forbidden, and Muslims are encouraged to protect themselves by constantly remembering Allah.

kafir (pl. kafirin or kuffar):

literally, "ungrateful"; disbeliever, one who rejects the truth.

kufr:

disbelief, rejection of the truth.

Mi'raj:

the ascending of the Prophet ﷺ into the seven heavens, which happened on the same night as the *Isra'*, q.v.

Mu'tazilah:

a sect which, among other things, believed in a third state between Islam and *kufr*, and that the Qur'an was created.

mufassir (pl. mufassirin):

Qur'anic exegete, a scholar who comments on and explains the meanings of the Qur'an. Many scholars have written such works, known as *Tafsir*. Famous books of *Tafsir* include those by Ibn Kathir, Sayyid Qutb and Maulana Mawdudi, parts of which are available in English translation.

Muhajirun:

"Emigrants"; the Muslims of Makkah who migrated with the Prophet ﷺ, to Madinah.

munafiq (pl. munafiqin):

hypocrite, one who pretends to believe in Islam, but does not.

mushrik (pl. mushrikin):

polytheist, one who associates others in worship with Allah.

mustahabb:

liked, encouraged. Refers to deeds for which one will be rewarded, but there is no punishment for not doing them.

qadar:

predestination or destiny.

Qadariyyah:

a sect which asserted that man had free will independently of the will of Allah.

qiblah:

direction faced in prayer. The first *qiblah* of Islam was Jerusalem, which was later changed to the Ka'bah in Makkah.

Rafidah:

a sect whose devotion to 'Ali 🏵 takes extreme forms, leading them to unjustifiably denounce other *Sahabah*.

rizq:

provision, sustenance.

Sahabah:

the Companions of the Prophet 🏵.

sahih:

with reference to *hadith*, sound, authentic. The highest "grade" given by scholars to *ahadith* that meet the highest standards.

salaf:

the early generations of Muslims, i.e. the Companions of the Prophet 🏵 and the generation immediately following them.

salah:

the ritual prayer.

shayatin:

(pl. of *Shaytan),* devils or disbelieving, malevolent *jinn.*

shaykh:

literally, "old man"; a title of respect (cf. Latin *senex,* from which the word "senator" is derived). A word used of a scholar of stature; one's teachers may also be referred to as "*shaykhs*".

Shaytan:

Satan, the devil. Also referred to in the Qur'an as Iblis.

shirk:

polytheism, the sin of associating anything in worship with Allah. This is the only sin for which there will be no forgiveness; if a person dies as a *mushrik,* he is truly doomed.

Sufi:

Muslim "mystic". Historically, Sufism first emerged in Basrah, Iraq, where some people went to extremes in worship and in avoiding worldly life. It is worth noting that the word Sufism was unknown at the time of the Prophet ﷺ.

sunnah:

the practice of the Prophet ﷺ.

surah:

a "chapter" of the Qur'an.

Tabi'i:

literally "follower"; a member of the generation of Muslims following the *Sahabah,* may Allah be pleased with them.

takbir:

saying *"Allahu akbar"* (Allah is Most Great).

taqwa:

fear and consciousness of Allah, piety.

tawakkul:

putting one's trust in Allah, relying on Him.

Tawhid:

the absolute Oneness of Allah. This is the basis of Islamic teachings.

ummah:

community or nation, the body of Muslims as a distinct and integrated entity. The *ummah* of Islam is not based on language, race or ethnicity, but encompasses everyone who believes in Allah alone and in the Prophethood of Muhammad ﷺ.

wajib:

obligatory, actions which must be done, as any omission is liable to punishment.

wali (pl. awliya):

a "friend" of Allah, one who is very close to Him. True *awliya'* draw close to Allah through sincere worship and belief, and their status as such is often known to no one except Allah. Although it is often translated as "saint", this word carries connotations that have nothing to do with Islam, as the popular meanings attached to the word have no basis in sound Islamic teachings.

zakat:

poor due, obligatory charity. A portion of one's wealth which, if one's wealth reaches a certain minimum amount, must be given to the poor. Percentages vary depending on the type of wealth (money, jewellery, livestock, harvested fruits and vegetables, etc.); in the case of money the percentage to be given is 2.5%.